DATE			

BETTER SPEECH
FOR YOUR CHILD

BETTER SPEECH
FOR YOUR CHILD

*by Michelle Lattman
and Antoinette Seandel*

 WYDEN BOOKS

CopA

First Edition

Trade distribution by Simon and Schuster
A Division of Gulf & Western Corporation
New York, New York 10020

ISBN: 0-671-22952-4

Library of Congress Cataloging in Publication Data
Lattman, Michelle.
    Better speech for your child.

    Bibliography: p.
1. Children—Language. 2. Parent and child.
3. Speech disorders in children. I. Seandel,
Antoinette, joint author. II. Title.
LB1139.L3L354   649'.1   77-15045

CONTENTS

For Marco and Jessica

BETTER SPEECH
FOR YOUR CHILD

It Starts at Birth

"How can I help my child speak better?"
"Is it all right to use baby talk?"
"Is there something wrong with the way my child talks?"
"What should I do about my child's stuttering?"

Being speech teachers as well as mothers, we've often been bombarded by such questions. Judging by the concerns of our own circle of friends and relatives engaged in the tricky business of raising children, we became convinced that there's a very wide audience of parents with questions about their youngsters' speech development. Our goal in this book is to answer these questions —to help parents understand how their children actually learn to talk and suggest specific procedures that will help their children speak better.

There's no end to theories that attempt to analyze how children acquire language. They all agree on one point: It's a complex process, mentally and physically. We feel speech is a learned skill. Children learn to talk just as surely as they learn to read a book, ride a tricycle, or swim the length of a pool. From the moment that wizened-faced infant makes his debut in the world, howling in vehement protest, he begins to go through very specific stages of development on his way to becoming an independent-minded verbalizing youngster. Just as baby creeps and crawls before he masters the art of toddling, so he also coos and babbles before he talks.

In our years of work with children, we've been very impressed with the powerful influence parents exert, wittingly or not, on children's verbal ability. They can affect the way children talk in a positive fashion; they can also create problems. As a result, many parents feel uncertain about how to encourage language without exerting undue pressure on a child. But once a parent understands what is happening every step of the way, she (or he) can approach the challenge of teaching a child to talk with confidence and enthusiasm.

The methods described in these pages will help you use the time you spend with your child during those first critical years to best advantage so that you can give him an early start in language learning. Your responsiveness to your child's verbal accomplishments at each stage encourages him to move on smoothly to the next achievement. Remember, it's you, in the role of parent, who'll exercise the most profound influence on your child's language habits. It's you who'll stimulate his desire for communication, model the vocabulary he'll learn to imitate, and choose the experiences you two will talk about.

Most parents would agree that one of the most important skills their children learn is to communicate their thoughts to others. But not everyone is aware that the foundations for *meaningful* communication begin almost immediately after birth. When you pick up your baby in answer to his wailing, when you smile back at him once he's learned to focus on your friendly face, you're establishing—right at that early moment—a sense of communication. As your child grows older, it becomes apparent that *how* he communicates greatly affects his achievements in a host of areas. Being able to express himself clearly is essential to his forming satisfying human relationships. Earning good grades in school is directly related to his ability to think logically and to articulate his thoughts with precision. Reading and writing skills are outgrowths and a continuation of language learning.

From your own experience, you've probably concluded that talking and communicating aren't necessarily synonymous. Many adults spout endlessly without making much sense. Others "talk off the tops of their heads." So, knowing how to talk isn't necessarily the same as knowing how to express an idea clearly—in short, communicating. You can help your child to think logically and to communicate his ideas intelligently at the very same time he's learning to reproduce the sounds of proper English. Vocabulary and thought then meld into meaningful language. Your child can learn how to organize and transmit his thoughts long before he takes his first public-speaking course in high school, *provided you nurture and encourage the development of his language skills.*

Language learning is an ever-expanding process that goes right on throughout adult life. Words and phrases go in and out of style with the frequency of changes in high fashion. New technologies, political events, even television patter nudge us to update our language constantly. Teen-agers are notorious for mangling meanings, but they also enrich our vocabulary with creative expressions and a vivid lexicon of their own, some of it eventually finding its way into Webster's dictionary. English is a living, hale, and hearty language. It changes astonishingly with each new generation. So, don't be surprised if the speech of your very young children is peppered with popular slangism and modish jargon.

When you are actively involved in your child's language learning, you quite naturally develop open and effective lines of communication with him at an early age. Whenever these lines don't exist, there's a problem. How often have you heard a parent confess, "My child never tells me anything"? Or a child complain, "My parents don't listen to me"? To guard against this kind of breakdown, parents must build a rapport between themselves and their children early on.

The responsibility for successful parent-child communication lies primarily with the parent; your willingness to listen to your child when he's very young helps set the pattern for a free interchange of ideas when he grows older. If you're too busy with your household chores today to lend an ear to his original rendition of "Goldilocks and the Three Bears," he may not discuss his social dilemmas with you when he's a teen-ager.

Communication is both an art and a skill. For some people, the ability to speak effectively seems to be a natural gift. For most of us mortals, however, the skill must be learned, practiced, and rehearsed. A new and rewarding dimension will be added to your role as a parent when you play an active part in your child's language learning. When you listen to your child with a sensitive ear, when you encourage him to express what he's thinking and feeling about the experiences in his life, you're developing both the art and the skill of communication.

You may be tempted now to turn at once to the chapter dealing with children of your child's age. Before you do, we urge you to read Chapter 1. The information you'll find there concerning some of the fundamentals of language learning will answer many of your more general questions—and it should make the section relating to your own child more meaningful.

1.

The ABC's of Language Learning

If you're a habitué of your local playground, you've almost certainly overheard mothers bandying about such pat remarks as "typical two-year-old" or "average three-year-old." Believe us, there are no such children. People of the same age do share specific traits, but it makes no more sense to thus categorize any age group of youngsters than it does to describe a "typical thirty-year-old." Every child has his own internal timetable that dictates his rate of development and allows him to evolve his own unique personality.

So many elements, so many imponderables influence his language growth! To cite just a few: the child's sex, his status among his siblings (if any), the configuration of his mouth, his general state of health, his degree of intelligence, the stability of his parents' marriage, the way his parents relate to him. Language doesn't develop in a vacuum, nor is it an isolated event, unrelated to other conditions.

The language experience of an only child born into a middle-class home in which both parents are college-educated would seem to be totally different from that of the child with three or four older siblings and a mother who's a high-school dropout and obliged to work full-time because she's divorced from his father. One might conclude that the first—the favored—child would receive more language stimulation and more opportunities to express himself. But that isn't necessarily the case. Even the most socially privileged child may have parents who are indifferent, or who are rarely home and frequently leave their child in the care of a baby-sitter. On the other hand, the offspring of the broken family may receive first-rate language stimulation from his older brothers and sisters, may enjoy highly supportive conversations with his mother, and may even have a rewarding relationship with his estranged father. No matter what the social backdrop of a child's life, then, parents can definitely create an environment in which language flourishes.

When your child is first learning to talk, you have an exciting, almost unlimited opportunity to advance his language-learning process through activities that will enhance the development of his communication skills. A child who's taught at home to use language with ease and confidence is being well equipped to meet the social and academic demands of school. And it's surely worth keeping in mind that a definite relationship exists between the ability to use language proficiently and superior cognitive growth and achievement.

The Mechanics of Speech

Speech is probably one of the most complex actions a human being can perform, requiring as it does the most precise mental and physical adjustments. Yet, we learn this remarkable skill at a very tender age. To produce the sounds that are part of the word he wants to say, a child must master the most intricate movements. Since speech is a voluntary act, we must be motivated to talk, we must have something specific to say. Although involuntary sounds sometimes accompany strenuous physical actions ("ugh" and "oof," for example), speech sounds are deliberately produced. Some knowledge of how speech is "manufactured" and the way sounds are made should prove helpful in enabling you to set realistic goals for your child and allowing you to respond constructively to any errors in his speech.

The physical aspect of speech begins with air that's expelled from the lungs by pressure exerted from the ribs, diaphragm, and abdomen. This air moves up through the trachea to the larynx, where the vocal cords are situated. As the air passes through the larynx, the vocal cords vibrate to produce the voice. The voice is modified as it moves through the resonators—the throat, mouth, and nose. At this point both the volume and quality of the voice are enhanced. Articulators—the lips, tongue, teeth, hard and soft palates—act on the voice to form familiar sounds and words.

Not every part of the speech mechanism is engaged to form each speech sound. Certain consonant sounds are produced without any voice. Vocal cords are relaxed as the air moves up from the lungs and articulators shape a stream of air that reproduces such "voiceless" sounds. Place your hand on your throat and say the sound *s*. Since this is one of the "voiceless" sounds, you won't be able to discern any vibrations. But if you make the sound *z* with your hand still on your throat, you'll be able to feel the vibrations of your vocal cords.

Each speech sound is produced by a particular placement of the articulators. Once again, not every articulator is used to make each sound. The *p* sound relies on the lips, and the *t* uses the tongue and a part of the hard palate just behind the upper front teeth—the alveolar ridge. There are three sounds in English—*m, n,* and *ng* —in which the nose is used as the primary resonating chamber. When such sounds are articulated, the soft palate (the back portion of the roof of the mouth) drops obligingly to allow the voice to pass through the nose. To a lesser degree, some nasal resonance occurs in other speech sounds. Place your fingers on both sides of your nose and say the sound *m.* Compare the vibration within your nose with what you feel when you say the sound *g.*

Vowel sounds are made by altering the size and shape of the mouth, and by changing the position of the tongue. Vowels and diphthongs (combinations of vowels) are always voiced sounds. Consonants are produced by modifying either the air stream or the voice with the aid of our articulators. Though the spelling of a sound may vary from word to word, the sound doesn't change. The eccentricities of our language dictate, for example, that the sound *f* may be spelled "gh" as in "cough" or "ph" as in "telephone"; the letter *c* metamorphoses into the sound *s* in such words as "cent" and "receive" or the sound *k* when we're talking about "count" or "arctic." It is the sound, not the arbitrary English spelling, that determines how our vocal elements respond. (How consonant sounds are produced is described in the Appendix.)

How to Set Realistic Standards

Young children learn speech sounds in a developmental sequence. Easy sounds are learned first and trickier sounds will be conquered at a later age. Among the easiest sounds for beginning speakers are the vowels and such consonants as *b, p, m, d, t,* and *n.* Moderately difficult sounds include *g, k, ng, w, h,* and *j.* Among the more challenging sounds are *f, v, th, sh, ch, s, z, r,* and *l.* Blends, or combinations of sounds, such as *tr, pl, br, st,* and *sw,* may also represent stumbling blocks for the very young.

As you listen to your child, you're likely to notice errors in the way he reproduces certain sounds and words. When your child "goofs" in his pronunciation, *be careful not to point up his mistakes.* Instead, let him hear the words repeated correctly by you. In bragging about his favorite shaggy companion, he may say, "Pitty dog!" Your response should be, "Why, yes, indeed, he is a pretty dog!" Don't try to force your child to articulate "pretty" correctly. In all probability, he isn't able, at this stage, to pronounce the *pr* sound combination properly. He'll get there!

Acquiring correct grammatical form is something that also evolves in a series of stages. If your child announces, "I goed to Grandma's house," you might reply, "I went to Grandma's house, too." Your child has learned to tag "ed" at the end of a verb to indicate the past tense, but that sort of common-sense generalization doesn't always work. There are the "went's," the "ran's," the "flew's" —*ad* insanity. (Forming plurals also defeats many a youngster, who may insist on "mouses," "gooses," and "foots.")

Resist the impulse to correct your child when he mouths such grammatical *faux pas.* Criticism may well prove detrimental; applying pressures, out of a well-meaning desire to set high but unrealistic standards, may lead to speech defects. A child whose speech never seems to measure up to his parents' criteria may decide to speak as infrequently as possible. Approval and encouragement, on the other hand, create a proper climate for your child's speech growth. Learn to appraise your child's ability, keeping in mind that his language should be developed to his full capacity, but not beyond realistic goals.

Remember, too, that while your child is learning to talk, he's also busy mastering so many other new skills—how to walk, feed himself, climb upon his stool, get into those stretch-resistant socks, share his playthings with cronies. Such chores may temporarily distract him from the business of language learning.

In addition, major upheavals in a child's life may send him into a verbal tailspin. Mark, a four-year-old, clamored for his bottle and his crib again after his baby sister was born. He forgot the rules of toilet training and, much to his parents' dismay, reverted to baby talk. His parents were flabbergasted when Mark, once a beguiling conversationalist, took to bleating "ba, ba, ba" when he wanted his food.

Mark's parents dealt with the situation by suggesting he might enjoy holding the bottle for his new sister-rival. They even let him try feeding from a bottle again. It wasn't long before Mark decided that drinking from a glass was, after all, more efficient. As his conflicting feelings were resolved, he discarded his infantile speech patterns and resumed the path toward maturity.

Moving to a new home is another traumatic event that may cause a language slowdown. Lisa, two and a half, spent much of her first days in the family's new apartment standing at the door, repeating, "Home! Home, now!" Her preoccupation with returning "home" to her previous apartment left her little time to talk about anything else. Lisa's parents tried to help her adjust by pointing out the advantages of her new dwelling: "Isn't it nice to have your own room now?" "Where should we keep the doll's carriage?" "Shall we get a pink blanket for doll's bed, or a yellow one?'' Lisa's unhappiness gradually subsided, thanks to such distractions. At the same time, the chance to describe her new preferences allowed her to enhance her vocabulary. With patience and an understanding of your child's needs, you can help create a secure environment. In this way, your child will gain the confidence required for proper language learning.

Hark! Hark!

From the time a baby is born, and perhaps even earlier, he hears a constant succession of sounds. Gradually, he learns to isolate those that are of concern to him—his mother's footsteps, his father's voice, a favorite song. He interprets these sounds through his understanding of the context in which they occur. When he begins to pay attention to specific sounds, when he begins to react to them, he has started—to listen. Learning to listen is an essential part of learning to talk because as a baby tunes in to the speech of those who care for him, he also begins to imitate the sounds they make.

Listening is more than merely hearing sounds; it involves concentration, understanding, and interpretation. We listen by screening out extraneous sounds in our environment and paying close attention to the meaningful ones. When a child is raptly listening to a story, he isn't likely to be distracted by the ticking of a clock or the sounds of a radio playing in the next room. The child who's about to profit from the words of his family and friends, his teachers and museum guides, must acquire this essential ability to focus on his listening "forces." We've included specific activities throughout this book to help children learn to listen effectively.

When *you* listen attentively, you teach your child that communication involves both listening *and* speaking. Demonstrate your genuine interest by looking directly at your child when he talks. Eye contact is important! It assures your little speaker that he has captured your attention. Listen *actively* to your child by making comments or posing questions—but do let him finish what he has to say without any abrupt interruptions.

Let your child be aware that what he has to say can get results. Grant his requests when that's possible or help him to understand why some of his demands can't be fulfilled.

When Christopher's outing to a baseball game was canceled because of a mild case of chicken pox, his parents found they had a problem. For several weeks Chris had had his heart set on the big event. When he learned he wouldn't be able to go, he was crushed. He used all his powers of persuasion to convince his parents to change their mind: "I don't really feel sick. . . . I just have a little fever. . . . No one will ever know I have chicken pox. . . . I'll dress up warm. . . . I promise not to go near anybody. . . ."

Christopher's parents listened sympathetically to his arguments, and allowed him to give full vent to his frustration. Then they helped him analyze the situation realistically. "It's really a shame we can't go to the game," they explained. "We're also disappointed. . . . What a terrible time to come down with the chicken pox. . . . But there will be more games played this season. . . . We can probably get tickets for one when you're feeling better. . . . In the meantime," they concluded, "let's set to work finishing that model airplane we started the other day." Effective communication between Chris and his parents helped them all to muddle through a painful crisis.

There are times, of course, when you just can't spare

a moment to listen to your child. He should learn to respect your involvement in other matters, to wait until you can devote your full attention to his needs. Try to revive an interrupted conversation just as soon as you're free, and to return to a subject you've had to postpone discussing even before your child brings it up again. "Now, tell me about your trip to the aquarium," you might suggest, once those dishes are scoured and the beds made. "Where do you think you lost your mitten?" "Why do you think Lee tried to push you off the swing?" Your child will wait with some degree of patience when he knows you'll unstintingly give your attention to his problems just as soon as you can.

How to Create Speech Models

Your child's ultimate ability to communicate is strongly influenced by your own speech pattern, the quality of your voice, and the content of your language. You're his first and most influential model. Using a tape recorder can help you evaluate your own speech. Read a short paragraph in your normal conversational tone, and try to be objective as you play it back. You're bound to be a bit self-conscious on first hearing your own voice on tape, but judge it with detachment for timbre, sound articulation, and the general impression it creates. If you engage someone to help care for your child, evaluate her speech as well as other areas of competency. Remember, she'll exert considerable influence on her charge's language growth. Try to employ someone who'll provide a good speech model and offer sound language stimulation.

Is your voice pleasant? The answer to that question can be critical: The tone and pitch of your voice set the stage for your child's language development. An infant reacts to the quality of the voices around him long before he understands any words. Your voice quality is one of the most recognizable aspects of your speech—it's as unique as your features or your fingerprints.

The reaction of others to what you say depends to a large degree on how you say it. A relaxed voice is more pleasurable to the listener; it's less likely to be "tuned out." A strident, harsh, or edgy voice creates an uninviting environment. Regardless of how absorbing your conversation, if your voice is unpleasant—flat or grating —communication becomes difficult. Your voice also conveys your feelings and moods. No matter how you try to camouflage your emotions through the use of words, your voice is likely to reveal your secret angers, anxieties —or your boredom.

If you decide your voice doesn't sound smooth and relaxed, try this progressive relaxation exercise. Purposely tense the muscles in your body, then gradually let them unwind. Start with your toes. Then think loose and easy as you let your legs go limp, next your torso, then in turn your hands, arms, chest, throat, and face. Feel your tensions melt away as your head drops. Practice sighing deeply in this position; you should be able to feel your throat unclogging. Holding your head upright, next, try yawning. Make the sound "Ah-h-h" and try to sustain it in a steady, smooth tone. Maintain that easy, open sensation in your throat as you begin to rehearse words—and sentences. You should notice an improvement in the quality and tone of your voice.

Do you speak with the right volume? If you feel your normal speaking voice is too loud, you can consciously make the effort to speak softer. Remind yourself to use less volume each time you prepare to speak. The relaxation exercise described above may also prove helpful in controlling the power of your voice. If you speak loudly as a device for attracting your child's attention, practice lowering your voice so that he'll really have to listen in order to understand what you're saying. Some parents yell at their children as a discipline measure. As a rule, that method doesn't work for very long; children soon learn to tune out the sounds of braying parents and may simply ignore their shouted words.

Pay close attention to daily situations that may cause you to raise your voice. If your voice tends to reach its maximum volume about the time you're preparing dinner and trying, almost simultaneously, to juggle a dozen other chores, try shifting some of those responsibilities to less hectic hours of the day. Bathing the baby after lunch, feeding the dog in the morning, preparing the evening stew right after breakfast—these could constitute changes in your daily schedule that would help reduce your tensions and lower your decibel level, along with your blood pressure!

A voice that's naturally too soft can also be strengthened through practice. Concentrate on breathing deeply, on projecting your voice, on using an extra measure of energy when you speak. Imagine that your voice starts deep within your chest and that you must propel it forward—with vigor and force. Be sure you open your mouth widely as you speak and that you enunciate with care.

Do you speak at a proper rate? Speech that's too fast isn't only difficult to fathom—it also creates tensions since it frustrates the listener. If your child seems to have difficulty following your directions or understanding your explanations, the problem may be that you talk too rapidly. Your speech should be deliberate enough for him to pick out the key words and to follow the main lines of your conversation. The expression on your child's face as you talk to him, along with his response to your words, should tell you whether he's following you.

Listen to your own words and try to imagine you're hearing them for a first time. Would *you* have trouble following what you're saying? Maybe you'd better slow down—but not, please, to the point where your speech becomes dull, plodding, or tedious.

Using a variety of speech rhythms (to suit the content of your language) adds interest to what you have to say. Obviously, when you're exercised over some matter, your speech rate becomes more accelerated than when you're issuing routine directions. It might be helpful to practice reading aloud from a book, after having marked the paragraphs to indicate where the pauses between phrases should go. Try to vary your speech rate to suit the material. Pace yourself to sound natural.

Do you pronounce your words clearly and accurately? Your crisp articulation is an essential factor in helping your child learn to speak correctly. As you listen to your own speech on tape, evaluate the way you produce sounds. If a particular sound doesn't seem to be quite right, refer to the Appendix in which each sound is described; then compare your way of forming the sound with our yard-sticks. Practice our suggestions while standing in front of a mirror. Integrate the troublesome sounds into words and phrases, then try to use the correct sound in your conversational speech.

Your speech ought to sound smooth and unstilted. Don't try to pronounce each syllable with equal force. In ordinary conversation, some words and syllables are stressed, others aren't. In the sentence "I want to buy a carriage for my baby," the words "to," "a," and "for" should be unstressed—that is, they should be spoken with less strength than the other words in the sentence. In general, pronouns, prepositions, and conjunctions receive less emphasis than the nouns, verbs, adjectives, and adverbs, which serve as the "information carriers" in a sentence. The rule doesn't always hold, however, since the meaning of a sentence is, in the last analysis, what dictates the relative amounts of stress for each word.

Changing the stress of words is an obvious way to alter the meaning of a thought or reinforce a point. Consider the sentence: "Your tennis racket is on my chair." You may choose to put the emphasis on "your," on "my," or on "on." Each variation subtly changes the impact of that message.

Your child picks up on these subtleties, so do try to use natural stress patterns. While making a walking tour of the zoo, you might be tempted to space out the word "el-e-phant." You'll be better advised, though, to pronounce such multisyllable words in a natural fashion; when a child hears syllabic distortions, he's quite likely to repeat them. Even though your child may not yet be able to handle cumbersome words himself, it's important that he hear them correctly spoken.

Do you use language that's appropriate for your child's age?

At each stage, your child needs a speech model that keeps pace with his growing skills, a model that's not overcomplicated for him. When you speak to your child, make an effort to highlight the key words in your sentences, those that convey your meaning. "Bring me the book" is one example of a concise sentence that's readily understood. "I'd like you to bring me the book that is over on the other side of the room" will be more difficult for the young child to comprehend. While he's still very young, keep your sentences short and simple; as his comprehension grows, your phrases may become more complex.

You'll have to establish a delicate balance between challenging and confounding your child. By asking questions, you can often test his ability to grasp your vocabulary and sentence structure: "Why did we have to put your plant in another pot?" "Where is the Phillips screwdriver?" "Why did the little engine try to reach the top of the hill?" Another way to evaluate your child's level of comprehension is by observing his actions and behavior. Does he really know where the pieces of his puzzle belong? Did he accept your reasons for not visiting the fair today? Can he follow the rules of a game once they're explained?

Do you use language that's informative and interesting? By using informative language you expand your child's knowledge and introduce him to a greater selection of words than he already has. The one-year-old needs to learn the names of the parts of his own body, the names of the foods he eats and the clothing he wears, the toys he plays with—indeed the names of all the objects in his environment. A four-year-old is already curious about abstract subjects. He wants to know how fish breathe without drowning, where the sun hides at night, why it only snows in the winter.

At all ages, comprehension of words surpasses spoken vocabulary. When a four-year-old shows an interest in how the family car functions, words like "windshield wipers," "steering wheel," "speedometer," and "brakes" should be used and explained. As your child hears new words repeated in context, he adds to his vocabulary—and increases his potential for absorbing new knowledge.

Speech Defects

Most of the errors in your child's speech will normally disappear as he matures. But persistent speech problems may arise and should be recognized at an early age. As with any other area of a child's development, you'll want to consider the norms for his age as well as his individual timetable. Naturally, a speech pattern that would be considered normal for a two-year-old would offer a valid cause for concern in a five-year-old.

The causes of speech defects can be organic or functional. Organic defects are caused by a physical problem. Functional defects are due to psychological problems or faulty learning. Some speech defects clearly fall within one of these two categories; others may share a combination of organic and functional origins. Sometimes the physical problem that might originally have brought on a speech defect will be resolved, yet the speech impairment may linger on.

When an obvious physical problem exists—such as a hearing loss or a cleft palate—a child should receive medical attention just as soon as the problem is identified. Immediate therapy may be indicated in some cases; in others, correction may best be delayed. Prompt diagnosis can prevent poor speaking habits from becoming entrenched, and, often, early intervention can favorably affect the prognosis.

Functional speech defects are far more common than those of organic origin, and their causes tend to be less clear-cut. Some factors leading to speech problems may include imitation of a faulty speech model, poor listening habits, the absence of motivation for communicating, parents who subtly encourage immature speech, or undue family pressures. Often a combination of such factors is to blame.

Therapy involves modifying the child's psychological environment as well as treating the actual defect. In diagnosing a speech defect, it's essential to uncover the source of a particular problem. Merely treating the symptom, without identifying the cause, can be unproductive. When there's a physical problem, such as a hearing loss, it should be treated before or during speech therapy. There may be a situation in the home that must be changed. Or there may be a mental handicap that must be considered. The best approach to any speech problem takes into account both the individual child and his surrounding environment. Two children with similar speech defects may each require different treatment depending on the etiology and prognosis of their problem.

Classification of Speech Defects

For purposes of clinical diagnosis, we often group speech problems under four headings: articulation, voice, stuttering, and language. Problems may exist in more than one area. A child persisting in saying "wion" for "lion" (an articulation difficulty) may at the same time be suffering from chronic hoarseness (a voice problem). A child suffering from cerebral palsy may have difficulties in articulation, voice, and language.

Articulation

Articulation defects are the most common childhood speech faults. They include the substitution of sounds— "thoup" for "soup," for example, or "baf" for "bath"; the omission of sounds—"tory" instead of "story," "tuck" for "truck"; and the distortion of sounds—when a correct sound is only approximated by the child. Time will often correct such problems, but more stubborn cases will indeed require speech therapy. The overall speech pattern and the degree of maturity of a child should be evaluated before therapeutic measures are undertaken.

Voice

Voice defects include shrill pitch, lack of tone variations, excessive nasality, hoarseness, unnatural softness or loudness, or just a plain unpleasant sound. The models a child hears must be considered in these cases because a child's voice may be similar to his parents'. Physical abnormalities, emotional problems, or poor articulation can also create voice problems. Medical attention is indicated in certain cases, and, if the need exists, your pediatrician can recommend an otolaryngologist.

Stuttering

Stuttering, speech that's nonfluent, is manifested by the repetition of a sound, syllable, or word; blocking on a word before speaking; or lengthening sounds. Stuttering may be accompanied by characteristic facial expressions or other body movements.

There are many theories about the causes of stuttering. Some researchers view it as a purely psychological problem rooted in the individual and his family relationships; others attribute it to faulty breathing patterns or laryngeal spasms. Still others feel the causes lie in brain dysfunctions or in attempts to interfere with the dominant hemisphere of the brain. There's no universal agreement about the causes of stuttering and the etiology may even vary from person to person. Some nonfluent speech, common in very young children, isn't really stuttering but merely a transient stage in their speech development.

Parents of stutterers should make every effort to accept their child's language with forbearance and to listen patiently without interrupting their child or helping him complete his phrases. A loving and secure environment, free from pressures or tension, is essential in helping a child overcome his stuttering.

Delayed Speech and Language

Speech therapists consider a child's language development to be delayed when his speech is substantially below "par." Their diagnosis is made by comparing the child's speech with the norms for his age. A two-year-old who hasn't yet uttered his first word, a three-year-old who uses only single words, a four-year-old who can't be understood by anyone outside his family circle—all these may be said to have delayed speech. Here again the cause may be physical (due, perhaps, to hearing loss or brain damage) or psychologically induced (as in a case where there are severe tensions in the home environment). The child's intellectual capacity must be considered as well.

Once the cause, or combination of causes, has been identified, appropriate remedial action can be planned. Some children just need a little (or a lot) more time to catch up with others of their age. If speech therapy is indicated, it's often necessary for parents to work closely with the therapist. Correcting some family condition that the delayed speaker finds intolerable may be all that's needed to remove the roadblock to his progress in speech development.

Evaluating Your Child's Speech

Although only a small percentage of children have serious speech defects, few parents are free from concern over minor speech problems at some stage in their children's development. A child outgrows most of these "problems" as he matures. Other problems may indeed indicate potential speech deficiencies that need to be identified, diagnosed, and, in some cases, treated. Here are some questions you can ask yourself to discover whether your child has a worrisome problem:

1. Do you have difficulty understanding your child's speech?
2. Do people outside your family have difficulty understanding your child?
3. Does your child sound very different from other children of his own age?
4. Does your child have difficulty understanding the speech of others?
5. Is your child unhappy about the way he speaks?
6. Do other children tease him about his speech or imitate the way he talks?
7. Does his voice usually sound hoarse, monotonous, or too loud or too soft?
8. Is there any physical or emotional condition that seems to be interfering with the normal development of speech?

If, after answering these questions, you feel your child might require speech therapy, referrals for a diagnosis can be made by your pediatrician, your hospital's speech-and-hearing clinic, or the speech consultant in your school system. For further information about the speech and hearing services offered in your area, write to your State Department of Education or your State Department of Health. The names of speech therapists who have clinical certification as well as a list of registered clinic programs can be secured from the American

Speech and Hearing Association, 9030 Old Georgetown Road, Washington, D.C. 20014.

We strongly advise against parents attempting to diagnose or to correct speech defects without seeking professional consultation. A speech pattern that a concerned parent views as defective may, in fact, be a temporary and normal phase of development; an outstanding example of this is the period of childhood nonfluency, an ephemeral stage that some young children normally experience. If a speech defect does exist, it should be fully and carefully diagnosed only by a qualified speech therapist.

A few more words of caution. There's a right way and a wrong way to approach a speech defect. If, at age seven, Johnny's still saying "wabbit" instead of "rabbit," therapy might well be indicated—but in careful stages. Johnny might be quite aware of his sound substitution, but still be unable to say the sound correctly. Merely telling him the correct way to utter the sound isn't necessarily going to bring about improvement. What Johnny may require is a combination of auditory discrimination, visual training, tactile experiences, and articulation practice.

A tall order, but what's involved is this: Johnny must learn to hear the difference between the sounds *w* and *r,* both by themselves and in words; he must see the difference in his own mouth as he attempts the sounds; he must train his tongue and his lips to behave properly in forming the correct sounds; he must practice making the sounds by themselves, in conjunction with vowels, in various position within words, in full sentences, and then in normal conversation. This plan offers a logical remedial progression, using a multisensory approach; it involves learning a new sound by breaking it down into various components; it's designed to proceed step by step so as to avoid overwhelming the child.

While your child is undergoing this kind of thorough therapy, your role as parent requires that you offer him full support and encouragement. Your cooperation with the therapist will be needed to help your child break his long-standing speech habit and retrain himself. Learn to face your feelings about your child's speech problem honestly and to deal with them openly. Is it possible you feel guilt about some episode in your child's earlier years? Do you feel embarrassed by his speech, or depressed about his difficulties? Do you worry that they won't be corrected? Do you blame someone else for your child's speech inadequacies? A conference with your child's speech therapist or even some professional counseling may go a long way toward ferreting out your best-veiled feelings and contribute a lot to your child's successful retraining.

Language Growth and Enrichment

The ensuing chapters, which are labeled chronologically, generally follow the stages of language growth. It's unlikely that your child will precisely fit the profile we've sketched in the chapter treating his age. To put your situation into clearer perspective, we suggest you read the chapter that precedes the one about your child's age group as well as the one that follows it. The first section of each of the chapters outlines the language-learning process; the second part suggests activities designed to stimulate and enrich language. These activities can become an integral part of the day you share with your child; you can capitalize on his enjoyment of language by using them to develop his verbal skills.

Let's say your child is experimenting with rhyming nonsense syllables. He chants, "Look, mook, gook." Well, you might just add "pook" and "zook." Jokes, puns, and riddles all contribute to the satisfaction a child derives from his mastery of language. When your child recounts his first "Knock, knock" absurdity, or when he badgers you with, "Why did the chicken cross the street?" be sure you share his joy at discovering these "original" comic routines. This kind of easy sound and word play also provides him with a solid foundation for reading accomplishments.

If you're sensitive to your child's burgeoning abilities, you can take advantage of such activities to help him use his new language. Following his nursery school's visit to a firehouse, for example, you might consider assembling a scrapbook with your three-year-old to help him recall the names of all that fire-fighting equipment he admired. Your five-year-old can be encouraged to pretend he *is* a fireman—you might write a little play together on the subject.

Any time that you manage to salvage during a busy day can afford a marvelous opportunity for language activities. While you're waiting for the doctor, you can pleasantly pass the time in his waiting room reading a story together. On a rainy shut-in day, a game of lotto or an improvised puppet show can be so much more fun than routine televiewing.

Which brings us to the controversy about the effects of television on children—a concern to parents, educators, and even those engaged in that awesome industry. Certain programs, tailored to the needs of young children, can have a positive effect on language and intellectual development. Still, you ought to preview such programs to be sure they're suitable. Familiarize yourself with the personalities and happenings on your child's favorite programs by sharing them. When you discuss what you've watched, your child becomes an active participant rather than a passive viewer.

Keep in mind that most television shows aren't benefi-

cial for susceptible youngsters, despite the shows' entertainment value for more mature audiences. Television
isn't only seductive; it can be addictive. The responsibility for monitoring your child's TV fare clearly lies with
you.

Nicole, a four-year-old, was housebound for two weeks
because of an ear infection. As her mother's patience
(and imagination) began to flag, Nicole was permitted to
watch more and more television each day. (Whatever
else you care to say about TV, it surely is an efficient, if
mindless, baby-sitter.) Gradually, Nicole's mother noticed that her daughter ignored her games, no longer
fantasized with her dolls, and had lost interest in her
favorite story books. The final blow came when Nicole
woke up one morning after she was well and asked if she
could stay home and watch television instead of going off
to nursery school.

Of all the things a parent is called on to do, one of his
most courageous acts, these days, may be to turn off the
television set when he doesn't think his child ought to be
mesmerized by it.

When young children have "nothing to do," they become bored, restless, and contrary. The activities in this
book can help you put the time spent with your child to
productive use. As you actively participate in the phenomenon of language learning, you bolster the foundation for communication. If you approach these activities
with a sense of enthusiasm and enjoyment, your attitude
is transmitted to your child. When you're tense or distracted, he'll be aware of your soured mood and react to
it.

Consider your child's moods, too; don't pressure him
to participate; you can always return to the activity at a
later moment. At times, allow your child to direct an
activity. Being "the leader" adds to his feelings of self-

worth and confidence. Follow your child's suggestions whenever possible and modify an activity whenever he offers a workable alternative. A child who feels free to explore various options is strengthening his natural creativity.

The starred activities at the end of most chapters indicate activities that are more difficult and best suited to the child whose motor and sensory skills are fairly mature. To the child who's advanced in his use of language, these activities offer a greater challenge. They offer parents the opportunity to give their child a maximum degree of verbal stimulation consistent with good sense. Use these activities as a supplement after your child has successfully completed all the others.

Your deepening understanding of how language develops will allow you to give your child a priceless headstart in learning how to communicate effectively. Your positive comments and frequent praise will show your child the pride you take in his language ability. When he's ready, encourage him to speak for himself and to express his very own ideas and opinions.

Let your child order his own meal in a restaurant. Let him tell his doctor just where it hurts; let him ask his own directions in the museum. Above all, respect your child's individuality. Read our book, please, with your child in mind. Remember, he's "typically" himself and can't be compared to any other child in your local playground— or in all the world.

2.

Getting to Know You: Birth to Six Months

Helene and Larry were looking forward to the birth of their first child with a sense of great excitement. Larry would often rest his hand on Helene's expanding stomach, and carry on lengthy discussions with their unborn child. The parents-to-be loved to speculate together about how handsome their son would prove; how kind, thoughtful, and sensitive he'd be; and what a fabulous career he'd forge. They had long ago agreed that their little genius would be called Bobby. It was an adaptable name, too, for if Helene's suspicions proved correct —and Larry was resigned to that possibility—the child would be Roberta rather than Robert.

Meanwhile, Larry went on extolling the virtues of the boy he was sure was "waiting in the wings." Bobby would have a powerful tennis serve—and a commanding intellect, as well. He'd be skilled in the musical arts so that there'd never be a need to remind him to practice the piano. As Bobby's "time" approached, his father went on to "discuss" ever weightier matters with his prodigy. Together they "pondered" such questions as, "If a tree falls in a forest devoid of all human ears, does it make a sound?" "How large is infinity?" "Is the theory of relativity still valid?" Bobby was always assigned some startling and fresh point of view.

Reality interceded with the start of Helene's labor pains. Bobby, it turned out, was twins. Now, both Larry and Helene were much too immersed in practicalities to decide which of the twins would turn out to be a musical genius, which a great philosopher. One thing is certain, though. The twins started life with a great plus: the enthusiastic attitude of their parents toward the practice of communicating. A zest for establishing solid human contact is the first step in forging the vital link between parent and child.

For the human child, communication may indeed begin even before birth. Already, in the prenatal environment of the womb, a baby's constantly exposed to a variety of sounds—the beating of the heart, digestive noises, coughs and sneezes. Even external noises may affect the fetus. Toward the end of her pregnancy, Janet often felt her baby move when the alarm went off at 7:00 A.M. Whenever she tried to steal a few extra minutes of shut-eye, her baby's kicking reminded her it was time to start the day.

The Many Messages of Crying

If a loud and lusty cry is the universal beginning of language, distinctive differences in crying patterns appear almost at once thereafter. You've only to peer in at a maternity-ward nursery to observe behavioral differences among even the tiniest lodgers there. Some babies vocalize with soft sounds; others cry havoc with all their little forces, and sometimes their entire bodies.

The cries your baby makes during the first days of life are a reflex action brought about by a stream of air passing from his lungs through his vocal cords. At first, there seems to be no real reason for these sounds, a fact that can contribute to a parent's frustrations.

Sylvia and David were constantly stymied when they tried to "read the message" of their infant son's crying. Sometimes they were able to still him by either holding or feeding or burping or changing him. Other times, nothing they tried seemed to console the child or still his voice. They did begin to notice that the baby's most urgent crying spell occurred at the same time each day, the family's dinner hour. But even when they arranged to feed their baby at that hour, his crying was largely unabated. After discussing this pattern with their pediatrician, they became convinced that there was no specific cause after all. David rationalized that their child was destined to become an opera singer and was merely giving his lungs a good workout. "It's never too early to train for the theater," he murmured philosophically as he adjusted his earplugs.

Since crying is—at least, at first—your baby's sole means of galvanizing your attention, he soon learns that someone will come to his aid if only he opens his mouth, breathes deeply, and lets the air pass through his vocal cords. As the weeks fly by, parents become adept at differentiating their infant's stock of Morse codes. Soon they can tell in a trice if a cry means "It's time for my nap!" or if it signifies "What's holding up my lunch?" In rather short order, you'll know when your precious one is hungry, or needs a dry diaper, or just yearns for a little affection.

It's amazing how much information your infant can communicate! Just as you transmit meanings by changing the tone of your voice, your baby learns how to modify the loudness, modulate the pitch, and control the duration of his cries. The sooner you learn to interpret his messages, the sooner the flow of communication can begin.

Some parents worry about "spoiling" their baby if they respond at once each time he bellows; they think that letting their baby "cry it out" is "good discipline." We believe that an infant's crying should never be ignored. It may not be appropriate to pick up your baby each time he cries, but there are lots of other ways to respond. You might pat him on the back, rock his carriage, sing him a song—or, better yet, talk to him. In addition to bolstering baby's sense of trust and security, your response convinces him that communication really works.

The Uses of Early Listening

Some parents worry that too much noise will disturb their new charge. That's not necessarily so. An environment rich in sounds is stimulating for a baby. When Stephanie's parents brought her home from the hospital, they took great pains to ensure her peace and quiet. Visitors were asked to knock rather than ring the doorbell. The telephone was taken off the hook while Stephanie napped. Conversations were carried on just above a whisper, and the radio and television were played at barely audible levels. Even her father's weekly get-togethers with his poker cronies were canceled. After a few weeks, Stephanie's parents began to chafe under their self-imposed restrictions. Unwittingly, parents can create an unnatural environment for their baby by drastically reducing normal household noises. Such precautions are unnecessary; babies have little trouble adjusting to everyday sounds about them. Indeed, a varied sound environment provides a baby with healthy sensory stimulation.

Even at an early age, you can tell your baby's reactions to sound by watching his movements. His response to loud or startling noises will be quite different than his response to soft, soothing sounds. The *br-rr* of your telephone's ring may cause him momentarily to arrest his body movements or to turn his head in the direction of the sound. His reactions, you'll notice, may not always be consistent. Sometimes he will ignore the same sound that produced some agitation earlier in the day.

How Swallowing Patterns Affect Speech

As a baby instinctively sucks at the breast or a bottle, he develops a pattern of muscular activity in his tongue, cheeks, lips, and throat—a swallowing technique that may last him all through life. This pattern also affects the way a baby uses the parts of his mouth for speech, since the same parts serve for both infantile sucking and for making speech sounds. Speech therapists find that deviant swallowing patterns are prevalent in persons afflicted with some types of speech defects. Babies who are breast-fed generally develop good swallowing patterns because they're obliged to work rather hard to draw the milk through the breast nipple and into their mouth; the naturally small size of the breast nipple also facilitates swallowing. Certain types of nipples used for bottle feeding also oblige a baby to suck forcefully to obtain his nourishment. Others, due to size or shape, may provide little or no exercise for the baby's mouth muscles during feeding.

The size of the aperture in a bottle's nipple can be of

major importance; if it's too large, it may force an infant to push his tongue forward in order to prevent the milk from rushing down his throat. The placement of your baby's tongue when he swallows affects the way his teeth grow. When the tongue habitually moves forward during swallowing, to avoid choking, his teeth may be pushed outward as they develop. Such malformations can, of course, lead to later speech impediments.

Thumb-sucking, too, can lead to the development of this kind of malocclusion and consequent speech difficulties. A number of sounds rely directly on the proper position of one's teeth for correct articulation. The *s* sound is frequently distorted among children with severe overbites, for example. In some cases, the child is incapable of producing any variant of the *s* sound and he substitutes *th*—resulting in "thee-thaw" for "see-saw." Both speech therapy and orthodontics may be needed to correct this kind of lingual-protrusion lisp.

Cooing and Babbling: How Sounds Begin

When, at about four to six weeks, your baby begins to make small gurgling noises deep within his throat, he may be making his first attempts to control the air as it passes through his vocal cords. As the months pass, he continues to experiment with such elemental sounds. He seems to derive great satisfaction from moving his lips, tongue, and cheek muscles, and these random movements enhance the variety of sounds he's able to produce. Your baby now begins to feel the new sensations associated with his mouth's contortions as he makes these sounds. And he learns an important lesson about himself—the parts of his body he uses for eating can also be used to serve a second function.

Before entering your baby's room, stop and listen to the sounds he may be making while unobserved. You may hear him say "Ah!" as he inventories the toys in his crib. He may offer the comment, "Ooh!" as he watches the movements of his mobile. Listening to himself, he's encouraged to continue making sounds. In short, he's fascinated with the discovery of his new vocal powers.

When Eric was five months old, his parents fondly recall, he loved to lie in his crib and repeat, "Gu, gu, gu" while he examined his hands. They remember the intense concentration and evident delight with which he "talked" to his own chubby fingers. Eric's parents would sometimes repeat the sounds Eric had produced, adding a new dimension to these sounds. Not only could Eric hear himself, now he heard others making the very same sounds. Repeating your child's earliest babblings provides him with an important source of language stimulation because of the reinforcement he receives as he watches your mouth and listens to your voice. Your response invites him to explore this new way of getting your attention.

Our friend, Marsha, vows she'll never forget the day her baby looked up at her and smiled for the first time. "The world stood still for a second or two, because now my baby was telling me he really understood I was someone special," she told us. This example of nonverbal communication marks the start of an interpersonal relationship that's so necessary for language learning. Her baby's smile indicated to Marsha that he'd singled her out from all other things in his environment; it marked an important step in his awareness. When your baby sees that you return his smiles, when he begins to observe your mouth as you talk to him, the visual components of language are being strongly reinforced.

During his babbling stage, baby usually experiments with a broad range of random sounds—some that aren't even used in our language. A linguist might pinpoint them as more characteristic of some foreign tongue, such as Arabic, Swahili, or perhaps Portuguese. Eventually, the baby must discard such alien and unnecessary sounds and focus on imitating those that are used in the language of his environment. By talking often to their baby, parents provide him with the information he needs to make this selective determination.

How to Start Language Stimulation

Mealtime may include six ounces of formula and one tablespoon of rice cereal, but another ingredient can be almost as important—a generous helping of conversation. Though your baby may not understand your words, now's the time for him to begin hearing the melody and phonetics of language. Tell your baby the names of the objects in the room; talk about the book you've just read, or even some piece of ripe gossip. Baby will eat it all up, along with his "din-din."

New parents sometimes feel rather silly chatting with their babies; they're self-conscious, unsure about just what the subjects ought to be. Your positive attitude and the sound of your voice are far more important than choosing the "right" words. Marty, a men's clothing salesman, liked to hold his infant daughter and tell her some of the highlights of his working day. At first he felt some embarrassment about talking to his baby of tweeds and blazers; then he came to realize that content was less important than contact. After that, he learned to relax and to go on glibly about cantankerous customers and clearance sale markdowns. Marty's conversations were, to be sure, one-sided, but his input was vital for his daughter's language learning.

Even though your baby can't talk yet, it's essential to

expose him to speech that sounds natural. When you're talking about that stuffed animal Great-aunt Matilda sent, call it what it is—a "chimpanzee," and not a "chimp-pan-zee." Exaggerating and slurring such great big words doesn't make things clearer for baby. It does, as we've pointed out earlier, present him with an incorrect speech model. The way your child learns to pronounce words normally is to hear them correctly spoken.

Much of what you communicate to your baby at this tender age is expressed through the quality of your voice. It's your *feelings* that are principally getting across now. On his job as a construction engineer, Frank had to use a powerful voice to be heard over the sound of the jackhammer. But at night his voice was transformed into a mild, serene instrument for his baby's sake. The men on his work team would have been shocked to hear the change. Baby, however, was soothed—and made to feel loved and secure—by the gentle tone of his father's voice.

The Power of Nonverbal Communication

Like adults, infants communicate quite effectively in a nonverbal way. Babies do it through body posture. When a baby's in pain, he may draw his knees toward his chest and grow rigid; a frightened baby turns suddenly or, if he's being held, clings closely. Look for the messages conveyed by your baby's body movements.

Nonverbal communication also occurs every time you pick up your baby. When parents at first feel awkward or uncomfortable about holding so tiny and fragile an infant, their tension may be communicated. As they become more experienced—and more confident—that sense of security is also transmitted to baby. At three o'clock one morning, Stuart was awakened by the sound of his daughter's cries. The baby had been teething, so Stuart recognized at once the source of her anguish. The only remedy he could offer was the comfort of his arms. He held his child closely, rocking her back and forth. Soon the baby calmed down, and the household returned to its slumbers.

Though you may not be aware of it, your negative emotions too can be subtly conveyed to your baby—and can affect his mood. Not surprisingly, then, on one of those blue days when nothing seems to be going right for you, your baby too is cranky. Phyllis started her day with an argument about moving to a larger house, over a breakfast of burnt toast and weak coffee. No sooner had her husband gone off to work, slamming the front door to emphasize his side of their heated debate, when the phone rang. Phyllis's mother-in-law was calling to criticize the way her grandson was being nourished. Half an hour later, the baby-sitter called to say that she was laid up with a cold. By nine o'clock Phyllis was a bundle of nerves. Now it was time to dress the baby. Phyllis's tension was immediately reflected in the way she handled her child this dreadful morning. Her habitually gentle manner was eclipsed by her impatience and short temper. As the day wore on, the baby began a delayed reaction to his mother's mood, becoming irritable, overdemanding—communicating his own dissatisfaction through his behavior. For Phyllis it was a day to remember—or rather, to forget.

During the first six months, your contribution to communication will necessarily be much greater than your baby's response. But remember, whenever you talk to your baby during this time, you're passing along to him your culture and your language. Along with the sounds and structure of language, you're conveying your con-

cern over his well-being and his security. The more trust-
ing, the more loving your relationship with your baby,
the more solid the communication you establish. And,
very soon, the more rapidly his speech will develop.

ACTIVITIES

Activities with your baby during these first six months are
designed to provide a variety of sensory experiences. The
input a baby requires to learn to talk comes by making
contact with his environment through different sensory
pathways. Try to imagine that you're weaving a tapestry
of sensations for your baby. The more variety you put into
it, the richer it becomes.

How to Stimulate Auditory Awareness

Spoken language requires the ability to discriminate between sounds. This skill is developed and refined
throughout childhood. At this early age, babies become
aware of gross sounds. It will take some time, however,
for them to attach meaning to what they hear.

Sound Awareness teaches a baby to focus on sounds.
Show your baby a toy that makes a sound: a squeaky
mouse, rattle, or wind-up toy. Make the sound and describe it for your baby. Put the object in his hand. If
possible, move his fingers so that he can make the sound.

On and Off helps your baby differentiate between si-
lence and sound. Place a music box in the crib. Stop the
music for a moment and start it again. When you're
singing, stop for a beat or two—then resume your tune.

Sense of Touch

Many of the impressions an infant receives about the world around him are transmitted through his sense of touch. Very early a baby reaches out and holds tightly to any object he can grasp. Notice how strongly your baby holds on to your fingers. When you hold him in your arms, let baby's hands reach out to examine your face. He may grab your nose and pull your hair with a painful yank. Your eyes and lips come under his scrutiny as well. Pierced earrings that he can reach become a real hazard.

Your baby gains some sense of his environment through the manipulation of objects. He's feeling differences in texture, size, and shape. Provide a variety of objects for him to touch. They shouldn't have sharp edges, be easily broken, or small enough for him to swallow. A small strainer, a plastic cup, a washcloth, and an empty box are objects that would make your baby more aware of textures. Give him one thing at a time. Run his hand over the object and talk about how it feels.

How to Encourage Visual Experiences

The motivation for language comes from what's seen as well as what's heard. Give your baby a visually interesting environment, but don't overdo it. Too many pictures and objects can be distracting. Baby is just beginning to adjust his vision to the world around him. A mobile above the crib provides something for him to focus on as his eyes follow the movement of the objects. Pictures on crib bumpers, the inside of the carriage, or the walls of his room also provide visual stimulation.

How to Use Your Voice

Talking to an infant is an important way of making contact. Just as holding, feeding, and comforting satisfy a baby's needs, so does talking to him. Let your baby hear all the variety you can express in your voice. Changing the volume, rate, and pitch of your voice stimulates your baby's auditory awareness.

Volume. When you change the loudness of your voice, you expose your baby to different auditory sensations. Crooning a lullaby can create an atmosphere conducive to sleep. Belting out that show tune while you vigorously chop vegetables communicates the energetic nature of your task. Try to match the volume of your voice to the activity.

Rate. Show your baby how the rate of your voice can vary. Count his fingers or toes, touching each one. First speak very slowly and then more rapidly. Exaggerate the differences between the two rates so that it's very obvious. Subtle distinctions aren't yet within your infant's grasp. Change your rate while reciting a nursery rhyme or singing. During "conversations," however, your baby should hear a normal rate of speech.

Pitch. Let your baby hear your high, squeaky voice imitate the sound of his toy mouse. Pretend your voice is a bass drum and "beat out" *boom, boom, boom* in a low pitch. Adjusting the pitch of your voice helps a baby learn to appreciate the flexibility of this instrument.

How to Talk to Your Baby

Let your baby know from the very beginning that talking is an integral part of your relationship. Tell him stories, sing songs, make all those silly noises adults make with infants. Imitate the sounds your baby is making as well. When he experiments with sounds, it's important for him to hear some of his "talk" come back from you, as already mentioned. You may even get a response as you repeat his sounds.

When your baby sees your face as he hears your voice, he learns to identify you as the source of the speech sounds he hears. Seeing you smile, scowl, look puzzled, teaches him—eventually—to interpret facial expressions. When he's about three or four months, you'll notice a definite response to a playful mood in your voice. Your "kitchy koos" bring a smile to his face. The fun at bathtime comes through in your lively, energetic voice.

As you care for your baby, take every opportunity to talk to him. It isn't necessary to schedule a particular "talking time." Associate language with every part of his day.

Feeding Time

During feedings—generally a good forty-five minutes —tell baby anything that pops into your mind. Describe what he's eating and how you prepared his meal. Talk about the culinary delights (pizza, hot dogs, Chinese food) that he can look forward to after his strained-carrot days are over.

For a change of pace, feed your baby in a new area of your home. This change of scene provides new topics of conversation: the story about how you acquired the dining room chandelier; the tough time you had choosing the wallpaper in the bedroom; your interpretation of the solid black canvas in the family room.

Diaper Changes and Bathtime

Babies love the freedom of being naked. Moving their arms and legs when they're unencumbered is a joy. Let your athlete know how much you admire his calisthenics. Tell him that they'll be valuable when he gets to the golf course or tennis courts.

Do "exercises" with your budding gymnast and tell him what you're doing: "Let's move your arms out and in." "I'm moving your legs up and down." "Feel your knees bend back and forth."

When you get your baby ready for his bath, name the articles of clothing you remove. Tell him what brand of soap you prefer and how cute he looks in his birthday suit. As you wash him, use the words for the parts of his body. When he starts to howl, apologize for the obligatory face washing.

Time for Loving

Talking to baby as you hold and cuddle him adds a special dimension to language. The warmth of your voice reinforces the tactile sensations he receives by being close to you. A sense of security and well-being is transmitted in this way. Tell him all those gushy things: how much you love him, how happy you are to have such a wonderful baby. The combination of your words and the tone of your voice helps establish the foundation for a loving relationship.

Too often, we fail to show our children how to directly verbalize love and affection. Using "loving talk" at an early age gives a child a model to imitate. When he's old enough to talk about his feelings, he'll know the words he needs. In this way, your child learns yet another use for language.

Time for a Change of Scene

New vistas await baby when you move him from room to room. An infant seat can be placed nearby while you're working. Describe your activities, solicit his opinions, ask questions.

Sitting on the grass with your baby can offer a variety of sensory stimulation. The sounds outside—birds, car horns, leaves rustling—are a new source of auditory input. Run his hand over the bark of a tree, let him feel the grass or a leaf. Talk about what he's doing. He won't understand it now, but later on he'll associate your words with these sensations. The more you put in at the beginning, the more familiar with language he becomes. The sound of your voice tells your baby you're there to share and interpret his experiences.

Other People in Baby's Life

A rich sound environment is created by the many voices a baby hears. Encourage the members of your family to talk to the baby as they look at (and hold) him. He'll soon learn to associate their voices with their faces. Don't isolate your baby; give him the opportunity to interact with others. This early and continued exposure helps a child develop confidence in his ability to communicate with a variety of people when he's older.

How to Use Songs, Rhymes, and Stories

Singing is the time-honored way of vocally communicating with infants. Choose anything in your repertoire—from lullabies to opera. Even commercial jingles with their bouncy tunes and simple repetitive lyrics are appreciated by your young audience. Personalize the words to any familiar song. In "Mary Had a Little Lamb," substitute your baby's name for "Mary." Change the words in "This Is the Way We Wash Our Clothes" to describe your baby's bath:

> This is the way we wash our baby,
> Wash our baby, wash our baby,
> This is the way we wash our baby,
> So early in the morning.

You might further improvise, "This is the way we wash his feet," or his hands or his face, and so on.

Don't wait until your baby is older to introduce songs, nursery rhymes, and stories. You can probably recall favorites from your own childhood. Many fairy tales and nursery rhymes have been passed on from generation to generation by word of mouth. Often differences in these stories reflect the culture of parents and grandparents. If you don't quite recall all the words to a particular nursery rhyme or story, by all means, improvise. When your baby becomes a parent, he may pass on your personal variation.

At this time, you might want to purchase a collection of Mother Goose. Although your baby is too young to sit on your lap and look at a book, use these references to refresh your memory. These books will be a treasured part of your library, and may well become heirlooms.

The Bedtime Book of 365 Nursery Rhymes. London: The Hamlyn Publishing Group Limited, 1974.

Marguerite de Angeli, *Book of Nursery and Mother Goose Rhymes.* New York: Doubleday, 1954.

Mother Goose, illus. Tasha Tudor. New York: Henry Z. Walck, 1944.

The Mother Goose Treasury, illus. Raymond Briggs. New York: Coward, 1966.

Toys to Stimulate Baby's Senses

When selecting toys, look for learning potential as well as entertainment. Try to find toys that stimulate your baby's senses. Keep in mind how the toys look, how they sound, and how they feel. As your baby gains experience with his toys, he becomes aware of the physical properties of objects. Tell your baby what his toys can do. Let him see you pound the pegboard with the hammer. Put his finger on the wheel of the toy car as it moves round and round. When jack pops out of the box, baby may focus on the lid next time. The ticking toy clock gives him something to listen to and see. Household objects—a plastic funnel, unbreakable measuring cups, a lid from a jar—are also interesting playthings for your baby. They're an inexpensive way of expanding his toy shelf.

3.

"Out of the Mouths of Babes": Six Months to One Year

Perplexities, befuddlement, and bewilderment—
such is the lot of parents during this period. Happy is the
mother who can reassure herself by comparing notes
with neighborhood parents. She usually finds comfort in
coinciding concerns. Does Ethan stand yet? Is Darcy
crawling? Can Ben grasp his bottle? So much seems to
be going on in baby's world during these early months!
Babies learn something new every day, they gain new
perspectives every waking moment!

One memorable day your infant pulls himself up on
his crib bars and blinks wondering eyes at the world
around him. When he begins to crawl, your home
becomes a vast laboratory for his research. Everything in
your child's path pleads to be touched and tried. Baby
rushes toward every object that rivets his attention—and
with astonishing intensity. The dog's water dish, your
pampered philodendron, become irresistible magnets.
His explorations are both reckless and indiscriminate.
He may even try to stuff his mouth with sand, cigarette
butts, and coins. If it's in his hands, so goes his infantile
credo, it's into his mouth.

Inevitably, he courts real danger. Parents must restrain him with emphatic no's. The complex stereo system in Meg's living room—with its battery of dials, its sophisticated and sensitive controls—proved to be a favorite toy. Meg's fascination with this costly sound system created a dilemma for her music-loving parents. Whenever Meg reached for the stereo knobs, they said "No!" and placed her in a different part of the room. After further investigation, Meg learned that everything in the room wasn't, after all, off limits. Wisely, an old radio was dredged up from the basement to satisfy Meg's curiosity about such things as dials.

In their intrepid drive to explore, babies have a knack for "getting into everything"—and especially things forbidden. To safeguard their valued possessions—and baby, as well—many parents confine their infants to playpens. The playpen manufacturers' lobby may file a vigorous protest, but our feeling is that restricting a baby in this way for long periods tends to cheat him of some very essential motor and sensory stimulation. And since he's out of harm's way in the playpen, there's a temptation to leave him there until he squawks his discontent. Clearly, a playpen has its uses, but you ought to exercise common sense about limiting its role.

When you do feel it's necessary to keep baby "penned" up, try to enrich his stay by rotating his toys as much as possible. Discovering the physical properties of objects—a rattle's clatter, the fuzzy fur of a stuffed Pooh bear—is a vital learning experience. Baby discovers similarities and differences while manipulating his playthings. So do exploit this natural curiosity of his, in order to make language building part of his daily routine.

You'll find lots of commonplace opportunities for enlarging baby's receptive vocabulary. In your visits to the supermarket, tell baby the names of the foods you buy.

Let him handle the cans and boxes. Let him squeeze those rolls of toilet tissue, while keeping a wary eye peeled for that cantankerous store manager. As baby juggles the products, associate each object with its name. Back home, talk about what you're doing as you peel an orange for his juice. Let him fondle the peel while you say its name. Make him aware that the fruit's edible pulp is found inside the rind.

Life can be much more rewarding when baby is permitted to pursue his natural curiosity. Once the obvious home hazards are removed, let your baby roam free and easy—even if this means you still have to supervise him closely. Take him along as you move through the house on your daily rounds. And talk, talk, talk! "Now, I'm going to make the bed. . . . First, I have to smooth down the sheets. . . . Now I have to tuck in the blanket. . . . How soft and cuddly these pillows feel! . . . Let's go into the kitchen now for lunch." What a pity if baby had languished in his playpen all the while, if he hadn't been allowed to share his mother's experiences as she straightened the bedroom and prepared the noonday vegetables.

Those Glorious Gurgles—First Paths to Speech

An infant's first sounds are spontaneous—and unintentional. Then, it suddenly dawns on the little fellow that his sounds relate to distinct sensations. A baby soon discovers that he hears his own sounds. Along with this auditory awareness, he becomes conscious of his own mouth. He relishes moving his tongue, smacking his lips, blowing bubbles, and causing curious sounds to be made. Unlike babies, adults experience their own speech primarily by hearing rather than consciously focusing on mouth movement. We have, perhaps, become desensitized to speech-related tactile and kinesthetic sensations; our rapid speech flow precludes awareness of each of the attendant physical movements. But when we do have to pronounce some unfamiliar word or foreign phrase, or when we struggle with a tongue twister, we can sympathize with the tough time baby has learning to use his own articulators.

Babies adore the sounds they make. This pleasure inherent in oral activities motivates them to keep on experimenting with new and tricky sounds. Before long, an infant begins to pair two sounds—usually a consonant and a vowel—to begin babbling "Ba, ba, ba," or "goo, goo, goo," or more ingenious combinations.

A repetition of these sounds intrigues him no end. By the end of his first year, a baby may link several sounds to produce something that resembles an honest-to-goodness word. He may even begin to string together groups of these sounds, indulging in prolonged patter as he converses with his Raggedy Ann companion.

Out of the mouths of babies—flow imitations! Your infant mimics the variety of inflections he detects in your own voice. His own tone of voice begins to assume many shades of meanings: severe and solemn when he appears to be scolding his toes; poignant and pleading when he's pushing for one more lick of his lollipop.

As your baby babbles brilliantly on, repeat his sounds. Note his radiant look of recognition when you "talk his language." He may even reply with another set of "Ba, ba, ba's" or "Goo, goo, goo's." During this kind of dialogue, your baby learns that others can also accomplish his very "original" sounds. Through experimentation, his repertoire of sounds grows until it becomes quite impressive. When you join your infant in sound play, you enhance this stage of his language learning. Your normal flow of speech, too, provides him with a wide range of sounds he may choose to imitate.

Baby Learns to Communicate

Have you noticed in how many ways your baby communicates? Though his vocabulary may be limited to babbling a few elemental "words," you have by now definitely established a link of communication. The telegraph lines are up and buzzing during this first year. You repeat the sounds he gurgles and he offers you his outstretched arms. "Pick me up, please," they seem to say. Play a game of peek-a-boo with your darling and you'll find yourselves sharing a barrel of laughs.

Baby asserts his individuality—his likes and his caprices—through this rudimentary system of communication. At nine months, Barry howled through his parents' anniversary party, forcing them to call an early halt to the noisy celebration. A younger child might have demonstrated his boredom with the goings-on by falling asleep. An older child would have used precise language to communicate his discontent with the crowd's breach of his peace. Barry, trapped between these two reactions, could only express his wishes by crying—loudly and emphatically.

Crying still provides the quickest and most effective way for your baby to command attention. But by now he has also developed a "vocabulary" of sounds. Just as you have learned to differentiate his crying sounds, you'll now begin to recognize his consistent vocalization patterns. A baby has his own code of sounds for specific situations; there's one combination for romps around his crib, a different set for bath-splashing time.

Sam's parents knew at once when his diaper needed

changing just by the sounds he made; they were quite different squeals from those he used to show his satisfaction while swilling at his bottle. When a baby is pleased with his rattle, tickled by a straw, kissed or fondled, his laughs and gurgles heighten the pleasure of these playtimes. How quickly a baby learns that his sounds influence adults and can contribute to increasing his own comfort! This rudimentary appreciation of the power of speech grows as a baby learns how language can be self-serving. Your responses encourage your baby to use language to achieve his desires. As he comes to realize that you do indeed listen to his wants and react to his "dictates," a bond develops between you.

Sign Language Works, Too

Gestures are a normal adjunct to speech. We shake our head from side to side in a universal signal for "No," *"Nyet,"* or *"Non!"* Your baby learns such gestures along with spoken language. Some he learns by watching his elders; others you deliberately teach him either as word substitutes or because they seem appealing. Andrea's mother taught her to turn palms upwards as they chortled "All gone!" once the morning oatmeal disappeared. Andrea, a born actress, used this gesture to enchant adult spectators. She used it routinely after her grandmother finished feeding her and once she used it to stun an audience of mothers at the playground after swallowing a fistful of sandbox dirt. This sort of gesture disappears once a child has learned to speak smoothly; others remain.

Gestures provide babies with one of their earliest ways of making contact. When he's had his fill of creamed carrots, a baby pushes his spoon away. Burying his head in your shoulder indicates shyness. Often a baby learns to gesture with his entire body. Whenever Brad's mother took his carriage out of the closet, his eyes sparkled, he broke into a broad grin, and he began to move with great energy. His actions spoke louder than his words. "Delighted you have decided to take me out for an airing," they said. Then, he'd begin to wave a supercharged "bye-bye," communicating anticipation and pleasure.

When your baby tastes something bitter, his facial expression conveys his reaction without a shadow of a doubt. When he's engrossed with a toy, his look registers deep concentration. Eventually, through observation and mimicry, he learns your own gamut of expressions. Your stern face may cause baby to frown; your smile can light up his face with a matching flush of gladness. Gestures develop simultaneously with spoken language in your child's communications growth.

The Lofty Role of Listening in Language Learning

When you hand your child a doll or a stuffed beastie, he listens as you say the word that identifies his playmate, and he associates the sounds with the object. With repetition, he grows familiar with the sounds and learns their meaning. Even though your child can't articulate the word "doll" yet, his reaction tells you that he understands. At this age, your baby has already acquired a hefty vocabulary of receptive language that he learned by listening. When you call him, he turns. He understands words that name his foods, his toys, the places he visits. If you made a list of the words your baby understands, its length would no doubt astonish—and delight—you.

Your baby is also capable of interpreting meaning by listening to your voice tone. Your no-nonsense voice warns him not to touch the hot coffeepot. When he's overtired and cranky, a soothing tone acts to calm him. The sound of angry voices may terrify him into tears. The sounds of music, of Daddy's carefree whistling or Mother's happy humming, provoke pleasant reactions. Other sounds—the whirr of a vacuum cleaner, the blare of horns, the roar of traffic—may prove upsetting.

Hearing loss can sometimes be detected at this age. If you find your baby doesn't respond to loud noises, to his name, or to your voice, he may have a hearing problem. The kinds of sounds he makes can also offer a clue. At nine or ten months, his sounds should normally be more varied and complex than those he produced at four or five months.

If you have any doubts about your baby's ability to hear, consult your pediatrician. He may refer you to a special hearing clinic for more extensive testing. It is imperative to recognize a hearing problem at this early stage, since the sooner a hearing loss is detected and treated, the less handicapped your child will be.

Poor hearing will impair your baby's language development, but even tiny tots can be fitted with hearing aids to mitigate disabilities. Special techniques for teaching language have been designed for the very young who suffer from hearing loss. Parents, too, can be trained to provide babies with special stimulation. Helping your baby hear properly is also helping him learn to speak.

Baby's Own Timetable

Some babies utter their first words at nine or ten months; others remain more or less close-mouthed until they're nearly two. By and large, these differences are without significance. Learning norms are little more than guidelines. Language develops gradually as baby masters the necessary combinations of physical and mental skills. Regardless of how old your baby is when he starts to spout real words, your stimulation will enrich the process. Comprehension precedes spoken language—and input forms the roots of speech.

When you say "cookie" as you tender your baby his treat, he learns the meaning of that combination of sounds. As he arranges his own sounds to resemble your "training" words, baby's babbling will flower into language. Soon he makes a sensational discovery! Others understand him when he pronounces certain combinations of sounds. When he himself says "cookie" (or some reasonable facsimile of those sounds), he's able to tell mother precisely what he yearns for. His earliest attempts may not sound like masterful rhetoric—even to a doting and indulgent parent—but give him time. His articulation is bound to improve. Showing your baby that you understand his dogged effort to communicate will boost his confidence—and encourage him on the path to real speech.

ACTIVITIES

A baby achieves readiness for speech through a combination of maturation and the stimulation he receives from the people in his environment. The preparation for speech begins with comprehension of spoken language. The language activities in this chapter are designed to maximize the development of receptive language.

How to Encourage the Understanding of Words

When you talk to your baby, try to speak slowly and single out key words for him. Say, *"Up* we go!" emphasizing the word "up" as you lift your baby from the crib. Repeat the word "up" when you're dressing him. Lift his arms and say, "Up!" Repeating words in their context teaches your baby to associate the sound of the word with its meaning. Use simple language so that he can pick out familiar words and phrases.

Parts of the Body. Teach your baby the words for the parts of his body by playing a pointing game. Point to your nose and say, "Nose." Point to his nose and repeat, "Nose." Reinforce the word by letting him touch your nose and then his own. Use this naming game for other parts of the body. Babies are usually most interested in the eyes, nose, ears, mouth, feet, and hands, although your child may be fascinated by some other part of his anatomy.

The poems "This Little Froggy" and "This Little Pig Went to Market" develop an awareness of parts of the body. Move your baby's fingers or toes as you say the poem.

This Little Froggy

This little froggy broke his toe.
This little froggy said, "Oh, oh, oh."
This little froggy laughed and was glad.
This little froggy cried and was sad.
This little froggy did just what he should,
He ran to the doctor as fast as he could.

This Little Pig Went to Market

This little pig went to market.
This little pig stayed home.
This little pig had roast beef,
But this little pig had none.
This little pig cried, "Wee, wee, wee,"
All the way home.

Where Is _____ *?* helps baby associate a name with a person. Point to Daddy and say, "Here is Daddy." Then ask, "Where is Daddy?" and encourage your baby to point with you as you say, "There is Daddy!" Use this game to teach your baby the names of other family members, pets, and people your baby sees often.

As baby learns to respond to the names of the members of his family, make the game more challenging. Have Daddy leave the room and ask, "Where is Daddy?" Give baby a moment to look around. Then have Daddy suddenly reappear and say, "Here is Daddy!"

Peek-a-boo strengthens the association between people and their names. Babies of this age respond enthusiastically to the element of surprise and eventually begin repeating key words. Hide behind a chair or his crib and say, "Peek-a-boo, Mommy sees you!" As he becomes familiar with this game, your baby may hide himself. He may even offer a "peek-a-boo" of his own.

Names of Objects. Your baby learns many words by listening to the normal flow of conversation. It's also helpful for him to hear words individually through direct language stimulation. Show your baby a familiar object and say its name. Let him touch it as you repeat the word. If the object "does something," show it to him. For example, show him a ball, and let him hold it and bounce it on the floor as you repeat, "Ball." If your baby attempts to say the word, repeat the sounds he makes.

Respect your baby's limited attention span; don't over-whelm him with too many words at one time. If he loses interest, try a different activity or just give him a chance to play by himself.

How to Encourage Tactile Experiences

The warning, "Hot!" is one of the first words your baby learns to associate with a tactile experience. There are a variety of other sensations you can iden-tify for your baby. Some of these he can experience by touching the object; others you teach him to avoid because of their danger. In conversations, use descrip-tive words to talk about the tactile qualities of objects. Take your baby's hand and guide it as you say, "The bunny is soft." "The rock is hard." "The bathtub is smooth." "The road is rough." Your child will begin to associate these words with the concepts as you con-sistently use them in your language. Use objects in your environment to teach your baby the vocabulary for tactile sensations.

Soft: pillow, blanket, stuffed animals, sponges, sofa, rubber dolls, fur

Hard: metal, tile, cards, doors, walls, wooden blocks, rocks

Hot: water, radiators, stove, light bulbs, a cup of coffee, electric heaters, sunlight

Cold: ice cubes, snow, refrigerator, ice cream, juice, water, icicles, air conditioner

Smooth: polished floors, windowpanes, bathtub, sink, drinking glass, plastic

Rough: sidewalk, carpeting, brick walls, tree trunks, the road, sandpaper

How to Use Gestures

Your baby begins to use gestures as an early means of communication. He imitates those he has seen and has been encouraged to use. Teach your baby to wave "bye-bye." Each morning as his father or other members of the family leave, take your baby to the door and show him how you wave good-bye. When you say "good-bye" to friends you meet on the street, storekeepers, or the children in the neighborhood, encourage your baby to wave "bye-bye" too.

As you shake your head for those many "no, no's," your baby learns to do the same thing. Because you put out your arms to lift him up, your baby learns to stretch out his arms when he wants to be picked up. Teach the gesture for "this much" as an answer to your question, "How much do I love you?" Baby responds by spreading his arms out wide. Use gestures as often as possible. They are among your baby's first attempts to communicate a specific thought by imitating your behavior. Later, he'll communicate by imitating your speech.

How to Encourage Identification of Sounds

When you talk about the sounds your baby hears, his world becomes a more familiar place to him. For example, you can say: "There's the doorbell." "I'm going to turn on the vacuum cleaner." In this way, your baby becomes aware of the many things in his environment that make sounds. He learns to connect the name of the object with the noise it makes. In the house, identify the sounds of running water, the doorbell, the vacuum cleaner, the telephone, footsteps, opening and closing doors, and the toilet flushing. When you take a walk outside, point out the sounds of sirens, the screech of tires, dogs barking, people's voices, and any other sounds you can name.

How to Use Picture Books

Introduce your baby to simple picture books with one or two objects on each page. Since baby's attention span is very short, show a few pages at a time for as long as his interest lasts. Start the activity by naming the object and pointing to the picture on the page. After your baby has become acquainted with the pictures, ask him to point to the object. Say, "Show me the dog." Guide his finger to the picture of the dog as you repeat the word "dog." When he's more familiar with the words, tell him a brief story about the dog: "The dog's name is Skipper. He has four legs [point to the legs]. He wags his tail [point to the tail]. He says, 'Bow-wow.' "

Telling your baby simple stories to go with looking at his picture books introduces him to listening for information. Remember to keep the story short; just a few sentences are enough. If your baby is distracted or anxious to turn the page, follow his hint. At all times, take cues from his behavior. When his interest is on the wane, go on to another picture or a different activity. These picture books are enjoyable for a baby this age:

Baby's First Toys. New York: Platt & Munk Publishers.

Dorothy Kunhardt, *Pat the Bunny*. New York: Golden Press.

My Picture Book. New York: Platt & Munk Publishers.

Jan Pfloog, *Animals on the Farm*. New York: Golden Press, 1973.

Garth Williams, *Baby Animals*. New York: Golden Press, 1973.

How to Use Poems and Nursery Rhymes

Your baby will enjoy hearing nursery rhymes over and over for a long time to come. Tell him the old standards, but introduce some new ones as well. Peruse various collections to find the strong, rhythmic poems so appealing to babies. Poems that are accompanied by physical actions are sure to delight your young audience. "Ride a Cock-Horse" involves large body movements. Hold baby on your lap and rock him back and forth as you say the rhyme:

Ride a Cock-horse
To Banbury Cross,
To see a fine lady upon a white horse;
Rings on her fingers and bells on her toes,
And she shall have music wherever she goes

Clapping hands is one of the earliest skills your baby learns. He'll have fun clapping as you chant:

Clap hands, clap hands,
Till Daddy comes home.
He'll bring some toys,
And then we'll have fun.

"Pat-a-cake" encourages your baby to pat the palms of his hands against yours as you say the poem:

> Pat-a-cake, pat-a-cake, baker's man,
> Bake me a cake as fast as you can.
> Pull it and prick it and mark it with "B,"
> And put it in the oven for baby and me.

The anthologies suggested here contain poems appropriate for this age. You might also visit the children's room of your library to examine the many volumes of poems for children that are available.

Marie Louise Allen, *A Pocket Full of Poems*. New York: Harper Bros., 1957.

Helen Dean Fish, *Four and Twenty Blackbirds*. Philadelphia: J. B. Lippincott, 1965.

Ray Wood, *Fun in American Folk Rhymes*. Philadelphia: J. B. Lippincott, 1952.

Ray Wood, *The American Mother Goose*. Philadelphia: J. B. Lippincott, 1968.

How to Use Music

At this age, your baby responds actively to songs. (During his first six months, he reacted to music more passively.) He begins to move his body to the rhythm, and may participate in the song by "singing" a word. When your baby is standing, you might sing "Ring-a-round-the-Rosy."

> Ring-a-round-the-rosy,
> A pocket full of posy.
> Ashes, ashes,
> We all fall down.

Encourage your baby to say, "Down," as he sits down.
Another song that encourages actions is "Pop Goes
the Weasel." Emphasize the word "pop" as you sing:

> All around the cobbler's bench,
> The monkey chased the weasel.
> This is the way the weasel went,
> Pop goes the weasel.

Music with a well-defined rhythm helps make your
baby aware of sound patterns. When you listen to music
on a radio or a record player, draw your baby's attention
to the rhythm of the music by clapping your hands,
stamping your feet, or marking time with a spoon and
pot. Give your baby a drum or his own spoon and pot.
He'll enjoy imitating your motions as he listens to the
music. When you move your body to the rhythm, hold
baby's hand and encourage him to move with you. A
professional dancer we know practiced dance steps as
she held her baby in her arms. When her baby began to
talk, he kept the rhythm with her by saying, "Cha, cha,
cha-cha-cha."

Many of the songs that would appeal to babies are
available on records.

The Best of Mother Goose, Merry Records, MR 6001.
Cock-A-Doodle Doo and Mother Goose Too, Recar Records, PCA 8000 QS2.
Lullabies, Happy-Time Records, HT 1008.
Mother Goose Favorites, Happy-Time Records, HT 1003.
Sleep Time Songs and Stories by Pete Seeger, Folkway Records, FC 7525.
Zoo Songs, Disneyland Records, DQ 1216.

Making Use of People and Places

Arrange visits with other babies of your child's age so they can crawl around together. In this way, your baby becomes accustomed to spending time with his peers. Watch babies of this age as they observe each other. They quickly comprehend that a baby their size is very different from the towering adults around them. Being with his contemporaries also gives your child the opportunity to hear the sounds they make, which so closely resemble his own.

Take your baby to the playground. Let him sit up in his carriage, and tell him what's going on and what's in store for him later, when he's old enough to join the fun. Experiences in the playground can help make language very concrete. Your baby senses "up" and "down" as you push him on the swing. Hold him on the seesaw and tell him how it goes "high" and "low." Sit with him in the sandbox and explain "empty" and "full" as you pour sand from one pail to another.

Exposure to a variety of adults is important at all ages. Language input can be enriched in the most natural way through contact with other people. Grandpa's version of "Humpty Dumpty" and your friend Paula's rendition of "Sing a Song of Sixpence" may be quite distinctive. Your baby learns that communication takes place in many settings and with many people as he observes you interact with others. Show your baby how he can share in social exchanges. Encourage him to say "Hi!" or to wave "bye-bye" whenever there's an opportunity.

Any new place you visit contributes to your baby's store of experiences. Tell him where you are, what is happening, and anything else that may be interesting. He may not understand everything now, but he's learning language from what he sees and hears. When planning excursions, keep in mind that it's difficult for a baby to stay put in one place for any length of time. A language activity can make any necessary waiting easier. It'll help distract baby, and help language learning, too.

4.

From Rattle to Prattle: One Year to Eighteen Months

Baby's first birthday is a memorable occasion, bringing excitement and happiness to the entire family. The birthday child may at first ponder what all the fuss is about, but pretty soon he's carried away by the effervescence of the celebration. The party hats beguile him, and the candle on his birthday cake seems like a magic symbol. If you're photographing the event for posterity, you'll find him a little startled by the flare of the flashbulbs. But he quickly adapts to it, realizing that this is indeed a special day. Your child is metamorphosing into a social creature; he's enchanted now when people respond to his presence and he's delighted to find himself the center of attraction.

A one-year-old can be a bubbly and charming individual with a great sense of fun. Little Amy was delighted by the game her baby-sitter had invented. The sitter would pretend to be engrossed in a book; then, every so often, she'd look up, fix mock-ferocious eyes on Amy, and say "beep-beep" in constantly varying tones. Amy, giggling mightily, enjoyed each repetition of the spoof.

One evening, when the baby-sitter was preparing her charge for bed, she pressed her finger to Amy's bellybutton and uttered a particularly ridiculous "beep-beep." Amy was beside herself with laughter. She never tired of her companion's game and, whenever her baby-sitter came to the house, greeted her with a reprise of that "beep-beep" ploy. Amy ought to feel grateful: Her sitter's antics helped instill a sense of humor in her and probably were instrumental in helping her master new words.

Though your child is rapidly becoming more and more involved with others, his philosophy of life at this stage is represented by two words: "I want." "I want that toy." "I want to eat." "I want to go up the stairs." He will never run out of wants. You may be sorting the dirty laundry, repainting the guest room, or concentrating on writing the definitive American novel—it doesn't matter. Whatever you're doing, it takes second place in your child's egocentric scheme of things. He wants you to drop everything to repair the broken wheel of his cart; or he requires a treat *now;* or he needs someone to get down his blocks from the closet shelf at this very moment. He's not yet sufficiently verbal nor sufficiently aware of the needs of others to consider any desires but his own.

One major compensation for parents of typically exigent one-year-old children: They're easily distracted. When waiting for some gratification turns your child cranky, divert him with some other activity. Molly's mother always reserves "water play" for times like these. Just when Molly begins to get irritable, her mother fills a basin with water and lets Molly bathe her doll.

Freedom to Explore: A Language Stimulant

Now that your one-year-old has begun to scamper about on his unsteady feet, he's able to explore on his own—and his curiosity has no bounds. He'll rearrange the shoes on your closet floor, rummage through the magazine rack, push all the buttons on the dishwasher. He's simply trying to get the feel of his environment; at the same time his enthusiasm for new experiences challenges his mind and spurs his language growth.

"Watch out!" "No, please!" "Danger!" "Don't touch!" You'll be using these admonitions more and more now that your child is walking. This is a trying period for parents; a one-year-old's knack for reaching potential danger zones far exceeds his understanding of the hazards he'll encounter. This is the time to "baby-proof" your home, if you haven't already done so. Electric outlets, breakable ashtrays, lamps, and umbrella stands all are irresistible magnets.

Out of sheer necessity, you now teach your child new language as you explain the dangers that can't be removed. Some parents feel a slap on the hand teaches the lesson best. In the long run, however, words are the most effective restraining force. When your one-year-old sets his sights on some object and propels himself toward it faster than the proverbial speeding bullet, words can reach him far sooner than your physical interference.

In warning your child of danger, be consistent in your language choice. Don't use words playfully on these occasions; let your vocabulary indicate you mean business. On the other hand, don't try to unduly limit your child's movements. Remember, a one-year-old's urge to explore is natural and boundless. All those gadgets and furnishings that you have come to take for granted are brand-new attractions for your child. Every step in a new direction provides him with a fresh experience—and the potential for learning new language.

Walking, then, is much more than a new skill. It's a liberating force that signals the end of an infant's total dependency, and the start of freedom. Moreover, all the energy baby has spent preparing for those first steps he can now apply to his next major accomplishment—learning to talk.

Imitating the Flow of Language

At this age, some children link groups of nonsense syllables whose intonation may be akin to language but which totally lack meaning. Such jargon mimics the inflections of language—perhaps the inflection of a question or the emphatic purposefulness of an exclamation—but there's little sense even though a real word may be interspersed from time to time.

A child's use of this kind of jargon represents his attempt to imitate the flow of language. No wonder it comes out sounding like a vaudevillian's double-talk! To the child, adult conversation must seem like a rapid torrent of sounds propelling just a few rare comprehensible words. To what extent children will use this type of speech varies: Some children develop very extensive patterns that they use for many months; others never do. As a child becomes more adept at language, the tide of childish jargon recedes; usually it disappears entirely at the age of two or so.

Babbling Sounds That Become Welcome Words

Just when does your child utter his first precious words? For months, he's been experimenting with a magician's bagful of sounds. Lately, those babbled combinations have come to sound more and more like honest-to-goodness English words. In fact, you may not recognize the precise moment of his first breakthrough into articulation, because his earliest words aren't likely to be clearly defined.

Ricky baffled his parents by constantly repeating, "Mamboo, mamboo!" At last, they decoded the message in that junglelike chant when one day he said the magic word just as he reached for his bottle. Having deciphered the word's meaning, Ricky's parents said the word "bottle" each time he was fed. Before long, "mamboo" had metamorphosed into "bapoo" and eventually it was transformed into "bottle." The way Ricky's parents uncritically accepted the word "mamboo" afforded great support for Ricky's tentative efforts to express himself verbally.

You can help your child when he makes a sound that vaguely resembles a word, by showing that you understand him—and confirming the word's meaning. If he babbles "pepa" when you hand him a pretzel, you should reinforce both meaning and correct pronunciation by saying, "Yes, here's a pretzel." Soon, the feeble simulation "pepa" evolves into a reasonable fascimile of "pretzel," especially if you reinforce the word's use by asking such questions as, "Did you like your pretzel?" "Did you drop your pretzel?" or "The pretzel is all gone, isn't it?"

When you conduct such a dialogue, your child soon learns that words convey precise meaning. You can see how the association a child makes between his use of words and the satisfying of his needs inevitably encourages language growth. Words help him, as he soon discovers, to get the attention of those around him and to satisfy his wishes, especially his hunger. When he pronounces the magic words "milk" or "juice" or "cookie," he usually achieves results.

Michael looked up from his crib one day and said something that sounded like "Ka, ka, ka!" His mother replied, "Car? Do you want your red car?" and with a big smile handed him his miniature Jaguar. "Here's your car," she said. The next morning, when his mother asked, "Do you want your red car?" Michael focused his gaze on her and repeated, "Ka, ka, ka!" Michael's mother was never sure that her child's first use of "ka" really related to his toy auto, or indeed if it had any significance, but through prompt reinforcement she had taught him to associate the sound with the object. And soon "Ka, ka, ka!" gave way to "Car, car, car!"

There are certain words that children of this age learn just because they're so frequently used in adults' small talk with their progeny. "Bye-bye" and "all gone" are classic examples. Your child will pay close attention to those words that are of special significance in his little world.

At a very early age, Karen learned to connect the word "coat" with venturing outside. Whenever she felt housebound, she'd say, "Coat!" Karen's mother came to understand this code word in very short order. At the same time, she realized that her daughter's language would not be expanded by hearing the word "coat" repeated in the same context. So, whenever Karen's mother was prepared to sally forth with her child, she supplied the appropriate words, such as "Let's go out now!", rather than parroting Karen's symbolic, but inaccurate, word-description.

Unlike Karen's mother, some parents fall into the trap of deliberately repeating their child's baby talk (or simplified codes), in their effort to facilitate communication. We feel that parents *should not* reinforce baby talk by repeating it. Rather, they should show baby that they understand his message—and then use appropriate words in replying. In this way, a child is reassured that his message is being received while at the same time he absorbs correct language. During your baby's earlier babbling stage, you repeated his sounds to motivate further word experimentation on his part. But now that he's entering his talking period, your child should be exposed to properly used language, even though he isn't quite ready to mimic your perfect performance.

The First Giant Step on the Road to Rhetoric

Don't be surprised when your child addresses a perfect stranger as "Da Da!" There's no reason to suspect his loyalty; he's simply using the word "Daddy" to refer to all members of the male sex. Not uncommonly, a child's first words express just this sort of generalization. "Dog" may be used to identify anything that travels on four legs —a dog, a cat, even a cow. "Truck" may describe any kind of oversized vehicle—bus, cement mixer, ambulance.

Baby's first words often express complete thoughts. "Apple" may well mean "I want an apple," or "I dropped my apple," or "Whatever happened to my apple?" When you supply the words missing from these terse expressions, you indicate to your child that you understand his meaning. You should be careful to reply in short but complete sentences. For example, "Here is your apple" stimulates receptive language and teaches your child how a whole thought may be expressed.

Any experience that leaves a strong, vivid impression on your child may also enhance word learning. One of the first hazards Danny learned to avoid was the stove.

As he played on the kitchen floor, Danny's mother frequently pointed to the stove and cautioned, "Don't touch! Hot!" Inevitably, Danny did place a probing finger on the hot stove one day, quickly discovering the wisdom of his mother's warning. The word "hot" entered his vocabulary at once, although for a long time it remained a generic term he used to describe any potential hazard. One day when he was about to pick up a bit of broken glass, his mother admonished, "Don't touch!" Danny looked up at her and replied, "Hot!" With more experience, a child learns to use words in a more specific way. Show your child you do understand him while he continues to use words generically. Don't *you* use general words, however. When you mean danger, say so, and when you want to warn that something is hot, don't use any other word but "hot!"

A One-Year-Old's Mastery of Gobbledygook

A child's early words are often garbled and veiled in mystery; only immediate family members may be able to decipher them. This is perfectly normal for beginning speech. As your child's listening ability sharpens and the movement of his articulators becomes more precise, his speech becomes more and more distinct. Meanwhile, tensions may sometimes mount when your child keeps repeating something and you can't quite fathom the point he's trying to make. Since his vocabulary is quite limited, close interrogation may only frustrate both of you even more. In situations like these, ask your child to *show* you what he wants. Pointing and other "physical language" help reestablish communications when words fail.

Some of Diane's words were readily understood by her

parents; others presented a puzzle. "Fu," Diane's parents had learned, referred to her cat, Fluffy. But what did she mean by "ort"? The "ort" riddle was solved when Diane led her parents into her room and pointed to the object she was so proudly naming—her rocking horse. A combination of guesswork and "show me" had finally solved the mystery.

Melissa wasn't as successful. She grew quite cranky when her parents couldn't even come near figuring out what she was talking about. She refused cookies, ice cream, raisins, becoming more and more outraged at her parents' lack of comprehension. At last her mother, having run out of other ideas, led her to the kitchen cupboard and asked, "Do you want a lollipop?" Pay dirt! Melissa's eyes lit up, and Mother tendered her the coveted treat. Melissa's mother repeated the word and pantomimed licking. She was teaching her daughter the meaning of the word and a gesture to suggest its meaning. If you can't discover what your child means, no matter how much you've tried, distract him temporarily —and try again later. Even though understanding his first words may present you with an ordeal, respond to them as best you can. And do take heart—your child won't remain inscrutable for very long!

Timetables of Development

Bruce, a bright young chap, began to say words even before his first birthday. His parents were thrilled to hear him spout "Mama," "Dada," "Pot" (indicating his terrier, Spot), and "Ony" (for his brother, Tony). Surprisingly, though, Bruce didn't add another new word to his vocabulary between the ages of one and two. He took to referring to almost everything in his little world of demands as "Uh!" When he was thirsty, he pointed and said, "Uh!" When he wished to go out, he went to the door and said, "Uh!" His parents were in a state of consternation over his lack of progress, especially since he had begun to verbalize so soon and so promisingly. When their worries became acute, they consulted their pediatrician, who assured them that there was no cause for concern.

Bruce's development was proceeding in its own particular way. And shortly after his second birthday, he began to discover new words again. Before long, he was jabbering away in full sentences. Bruce's case may be typical of many children whose language progress doesn't follow a smooth, predictable upward line. Often, language growth appears to occur in spurts. However, even while Bruce wasn't overtly expanding his vocabulary, he was continually learning language by absorbing what was spoken in his presence.

Speech learning can be very subtle. Children don't necessarily progress overtly from individual words to short phrases and then on to sentences. Some may appear to skip a stage in language development, although an evolution is really taking place. The child who leaps from individual words to full sentences "overnight" has been internalizing much of his language education. In all likelihood, he did go through a stage when he spoke in phrases—but for so short a time that it was imperceptible to his parents.

When a child's performance doesn't measure up to his parents' expectations, problems may arise. It's easy enough to pay lip service to the very valid theory of individual differences in language evolvement, but when your neighbor's child begins to talk and yours hasn't, your anguish is difficult to conceal. "I did everything the books told me to," you may rationalize, "so why isn't my child talking like Margie's?"

The danger lies in transmitting that concern to your child. Trying to impose language learning by making blunt demands or dangling a cookie before your child until he utters the word are no ways to help him learn. You do help if you repeat the word "cookie" as you hand it to him. Accept whatever means he chooses to express his needs; communication is far more important at this age than the mastery of individual words. Speech is a difficult enough accomplishment without adding pressures to the learning process.

At times, you may be eager to show off your child's verbal agility in the presence of some interested listener. More than likely, your star performer will then clam up as soon as he finds himself on display. Don't push or prod him. At this age, a child generally speaks only when he wants to. No amount of cajoling can get him to utter a single word. He's just beginning to understand his own capacity to say words others understand—and you, his parents, are those "others" in his life, at least for the moment. So do cater to his exigencies by adopting a relaxed attitude, one that will motivate him to expand his "conversation." When he says, "googie," or "og," show him you understand. You might point to the dog and say, "Dog," and pet it. Since your concrete reaction to his early attempts at speech gives him confidence, make every effort to show him how well you understand his verbal messages through such means.

Monitoring Your Own Speech

Speech that's readily understood facilitates language learning. Listen to your own speech and be aware of how it sounds. If you recognize that you speak too rapidly, try to slow down, but without sacrificing your natural intonation. Place key words—those your child is most likely to recognize—at the beginning or end of each of your sentences. You might choose to say, "We are going out" rather than "Let's go out for a nice long walk—it's such a sunny day." Similarly, "Time for your bath" is more concise, cogent, and conducive to response than "I want to give you a bath now so you will be nice and clean when Daddy comes home." Let your child observe your face as you speak to him. Watching the movements of your mouth reinforces what he hears. Your facial expressions give him additional clues to the feelings behind your words.

Language Begins with Concrete Experiences

To a one-year-old, "Up!" usually means one thing— "Pick me up!" Such abstractions as "up in the air" or "it's up to you" or "your time is up" have no meaning for him. A one-year-old's vocabulary is limited to the specific experiences in which he's directly involved. In an elevator, the word "push" takes on real meaning for your child only when you tell him to push the up button and he then feels the elevator moving upward. If you rivet his attention to the flashing numbers over the elevator door, and tell him what they represent, those digits too will eventually have meaning for him. In the same way, the words "open" and "close" take on significance when you use them to describe the action of the elevator door.

Allowing your child to experience things firsthand as you explain them will make his language more concrete. Let him help you to sort out the clothes for the laundry. Tell him which belong to Daddy and Mommy, and which are his. Let him help you pour the soap flakes into the washing machine. You make the words "Pull the knob" very vivid by giving him this instruction and then letting him watch the machine grind into action.

Your child has an enormous capacity for learning, and your input will help him to acquire a large portion of his knowledge. The activities described in this chapter are designed to take full advantage of a one-year-old's natural curiosity. They provide opportunities for him to use the words he has mastered and to increase his vocabulary. Remember when you plan your joint activities that your one-year-old's attention span is limited. There's no need to pressure him; he's sure to let you know when he's had enough. But even five minutes of language activity can be productive. Indeed, frequent short periods of "instruction" can be more effective than more prolonged stretches. Whenever you can, talk to your child. Soon, he'll be talking to you.

ACTIVITIES

How to Use Toys

When you participate in your child's play with toys, the toys can become vehicles for language learning. They can be used to introduce concepts, encourage imagination, and develop physical abilities. Playing with toys can help reinforce the words your child has begun to say and stimulate new language.

Your child's toys need not be fancy or complicated. Nor is "store bought" always a guarantee that the toy is appropriate or sturdy. When buying toys, don't assume that if they're labeled "One to Four Years," they're suitable for a child who falls within that age range. The span recommended for toys tends to be rather broad. Examine the toy yourself and base your decision on its play and learning potential. Even though a commercial toy is designed and marketed by professionals, that doesn't necessarily mean it's suitable for your child.

As an alternative to buying toys, try to find someone whose child has outgrown toys that would be appropriate for your child. If the car's paint is chipped or the fender is dented, chances are your child will love it anyway. The toy industry may not approve, but this course makes sense for the burdened consumer.

Dolls. A great deal of language can be learned through play with dolls. As you and your child play with them, talk about parts of the body, physical actions, and articles of clothing. When you help undress the doll for its bath, describe what you're doing. You might say such things as: "Let's take the shoes off the doll's feet." "Stretch out the doll's legs so we can take off his pants." "Let's wash your doll's hair." Your child can also learn the words that describe how people are feeling in this kind of play: "Your baby is tired, let's put her to sleep." Or, "Let's find your doll's bottle. She must be hungry."

Animal Toys. Toy animals help your child learn the names of animals and their sounds. Even though a dog and cat both have four legs, a tail and similar body shapes, you can tell your child about the differences in their names and the sounds they make. Encourage him to say the animal sounds when you ask, "What does the cat [or dog] say?" The sounds of "meow" and "bow-wow" are easy for young children to imitate.

Cars and Trucks. A child's fascination for turning wheels goes on for many years. His vocabulary grows as he learns to identify a tractor, fire engine, motorcycle, derrick, dump truck, bus, ambulance, and police car. When you play with these toys, use their specific names rather than just calling them "cars" or "trucks." Say, "Let's take the tractor and the fire engine out of the garage," for instance, or, "Let's load the blocks on the dump truck." To help your child become familiar with the names of the vehicles, play an identification game. Tell him, "Bring me the motorcycle," or, "Bring me the school bus."

Blocks. Children seem to be natural builders. They enjoy placing objects on top of one other and knocking them down. As you build with your child, use such descriptive words as "on top," "next to," "tall," "small," and "colors." This will introduce your child to a number of spatial and physical concepts. A set of wooden blocks is a blue-chip investment because children continue to play with them for a long time. As they get older, the way they use the blocks changes. A one-year-old may place just a few blocks on top of one another and then knock them down. A two-year-old loves to erect towers. At three, a child may place the blocks end on end across the room to construct a superhighway for his toy cars. When he's four, he builds his highway and adds bridges, tunnels, and skyscrapers. Blocks, or any toys with pieces that can be arranged and rearranged, are never boring. They provide a wonderful outlet for a child's creativity and imagination.

Every Body Part Helps

Where is your ———? teaches your child that his body is made up of individual parts. First ask him to point to those parts of his body you're fairly sure he knows: "Where is your nose?" "Where are your eyes?" If he doesn't respond, guide his hand to the right place and repeat the word. You help him learn to locate his tummy, toes, neck, or other parts of his body in this way. For a new perspective you can also play this game in front of a mirror. He'll be able to watch his mirror image locate the parts of the body.

A doll or stuffed animal with clearly defined body parts is useful for teaching your child about the body. Play, "Where is your doll's ———?" in order to reinforce concepts he's ready to learn.

Where does it belong? teaches your child the location of parts of the body. Dolls or other figures that have removable parts are a good teaching tool. Children enjoy placing things on and taking them off. Ask your child, "Where does the hair belong?" or "Where do the ears belong?"

You can also make your own toy for this activity. Use a potato, orange, or apple as a head. Draw features on cardboard, cut them out, and then attach each feature to a toothpick. Guide your child's hand so he places the feature on the correct spot on the head. Push the toothpick through the head to secure the feature and describe the place where you put it: "The nose belongs on the face," for example, or, "The hair belongs on top of the head."

How to Use Songs and Poems

Now that your child can say a few words, songs and poems are even more fun. Substitute your child's name, his pet's name, a favorite food, or a special toy whenever you can in a song. Add physical actions; they heighten his appreciation of the rhythm and content of the material. Sit on the floor with your toddler as you listen to a song on the record player or as you sing together. He's your best audience and won't know if you're off key or forget a word or two. Chances are, he can't carry a tune either.

Gradually, he'll learn the words to some of his favorite tunes.

Songs that involve action or tell a simple story are good choices. Swaying to the rhythm of the music, clapping your hands, or stamping your feet intensifies the experience. Improvise finger movements or use large body movements to further illustrate what the words are saying. Jump up and down together as you say, "Jack Be Nimble." Rock back and forth as you recite, "Hickory-Dickory-Dock." Pretend to hold a baby in your arms as you sing, "Rock-a-Bye-Baby." Gallop on your make-believe horse as you say, "Yankee Doodle."

Show your child the motions used for rowing a boat. Do these motions in time to the rhythm as you sing:

> Row, row, row your boat,
> Gently down the stream,
> Merrily, merrily, merrily, merrily,
> Life is but a dream.

Children of this age can participate in the song "London Bridge." Two adults can form either side of the bridge and your child can walk round and round as you all sing:

> London Bridge is falling down,
> Falling down, falling down,
> London Bridge is falling down,
> My fair lady.

In the next verse, the adults join hands, palm to palm, to form a bridge as your child walks through:

> London Bridge is all built up,
> All built up, all built up,

London Bridge is all built up,
My fair lady.

As you say the final verse, "lock" him in your arms and rock him back and forth:

Take the key and lock her up,
Lock her up, lock her up,
Take the key and lock her up,
My fair lady.

Encourage your child to use movements that involve his whole body. Smaller movements are probably beyond his ability, although he enjoys watching your hand motions as you do "Eensy Weensy Spider" and "Where Is Thumbkin?" When you recite, "Open, Shut Them," your one-year-old might be able to clap his hands with you or imitate some of the other actions:

Open, shut them.
Open, shut them.
Give a little clap.
Open, shut them.
Open, shut them.
Put them in your lap.

Creep them, creep them, creep them,
Way up to your chin.
Open up your little mouth,
But do not let them in.

Your child will enjoy moving his body and perhaps singing along as he listens to the following records:

Farmyard Fun Songs and Other Animal Songs, Happy-Time Records, HT 1032.

Let's Go to the Zoo, Peter Rabbit Records, K-21.
Little Toot, Happy-Time Records, HT 1015.
Little White Duck, Golden Records, LP 261.
Mother Goose, Golden Records, GLP 12.
Mother Goose Storybook, Peter Rabbit Records, K-19.

How to Use Stories

Children of this age are able to listen to very short stories while looking at colorful illustrations. If the text is too complicated, you'll have to make up your own version of the story. A picture of a cow and a sheep in the pasture is enough to create a story: "The cow and the sheep live on a farm. They like to be out in the sun. The cow says, 'Moo,' and the sheep says, 'Baa.' " These few sentences should hold your toddler's interest.

After you tell the story, encourage your child to use language by asking questions like: "Where does the cow live?" "Where does the sheep live?" "What does the cow say?" "What does the sheep say?" If your child doesn't respond to the questions, tell him the answers. The more he hears such stories, the more familiar he becomes with language, and soon he'll be able to participate more actively in the storytelling.

All kinds of pictures from books, magazines, or posters can be used for storytelling. This story may be suggested by a picture of a train on the railroad tracks: "The train is moving very fast. The whistle says, 'Woo, woo!' The wheels turn round and round." Then ask your child, "What does the train whistle say?" or "How do the wheels turn?" Use picture books to elicit language and to teach new words and concepts. But although your child learns a great deal from storytelling, the emphasis should be on the sheer pleasure of this activity. Some picture-book suggestions follow:

Dick Bruna, *The Fish.* Toronto: Methuen Children's Books Limited, 1975.

John Burningham, *The Baby.* New York: Thomas Y. Crowell, 1974.

Eric Carle, *Walter the Baker.* New York: Alfred A. Knopf, 1972.

Farm Animals. New York: Grosset & Dunlap, 1975.

John S. Goodall, *The Adventures of Paddy Pork.* New York: Harcourt, Brace & World, 1968.

C. Howard, *Mom and Me.* New York: Grosset & Dunlap, 1975.

Ruth Krauss, *I Can Fly.* New York: Golden Press, 1958.

Peter Lippman, *Busy Wheels.* New York: Random House, 1973.

Arnold Lobel, *The Comic Adventures of Old Mother Hubbard and Her Dog.* Scarsdale, N.Y.: Bradbury Press, 1968.

Ole Rison, *I Am a Kitten.* New York: Golden Press, 1975.

Yakata Sugita, *Goodnight 1,2,3.* New York: Scroll Press, 1971.

Garth Williams, *Three Bedtime Stories.* New York: Golden Press, 1973.

Pat and Eve Witte, *Who Lives Here?* New York: Golden Press, 1961.

How to Use Play Experiences

Your child needs play time with other children—in their house and his. He responds to the other children's company and begins to form relationships. Limit your guest list to one or two children at a time. Since one-year-olds do need adult supervision, you'll want to stay with the children as they play and give help when needed. Plan the length of time the children spend together. Keep the visits pleasant and fairly short, so the children don't get overtired. You can do some of the things already mentioned, such as read a story, listen to records, or play with blocks. If you include lunch, introduce sentences that reinforce the language your child is learning: "Give me your cup." "Here's your sandwich." "Wipe your hand with the napkin."

Going to someone else's house exposes your child to a different environment and new language. His friend may have toys, pets, or siblings that your child doesn't have. The type of home where his friend lives may be different from yours. A ride in an elevator can be a unique experience for a child who lives in a one-family house.

If you don't know any children your child's age, the playground is the obvious place to meet them. The park bench has been the start of many friendships as well as one of the best sources of information. Shared experiences about bedtime, eating, and toilet training help lessen some of the isolation and uncertainty of child rearing. Many mothers will welcome your invitation to have their children play with yours. And, you yourself might also make a new friend.

When You're Going Places

Even though your child is still very young, he's learning to operate in an adult world. He can walk by himself for short distances, drink from a cup, feed himself with his fingers, stay awake for longer periods of time, and say a few words. These skills enable you to take your child to places you might not have considered before, providing you're aware of certain limitations. A meal in a restaurant is a possibility. Select a place you know welcomes children (usually indicated by the availability of high chairs or booster seats). Taking your child to an "adults only" eatery can be disastrous for you as well as for the other patrons. Choose a time when you think your child won't be cranky or tired. At the restaurant, minimize the risk of accidents by placing glasses, dishes, and other breakables out of reach. Bring along a toy to amuse your child while you wait to be served.

Make this visit a language-learning experience too. You can avail yourself of the opportunity to introduce your budding gourmet to the words associated with a restaurant, such as menu, waitress, cook, dessert, breadsticks, and others. Describe what is happening: "Here comes the waitress with the menu." "I think I'll have a 'bimboburger' and a soda." "Could we please have the check?" A meal in a restaurant with a one-year-old isn't the most elegant or relaxing way to dine, but as you continue taking your child to places such as restaurants, he becomes accustomed to the special behavior required there and learns the specific language to use.

In a short visit to a department store there are also many things for a child to see, sounds to hear, and language to learn. He listens as you talk to the salesperson. All those playthings in the toy department are a feast for his eyes. He carries the bag containing his new car and will tell Daddy later about his new toy. When the department store guard says hello to him, he may wave and say, "Hi!"

Going places and meeting people enlarges your child's

view of the world and offers unique language-learning opportunities. Don't wait until he's older; start taking him with you now. There's a great deal to learn and it takes time to learn it.

ADVANCED ACTIVITIES

*Puzzles

Introduce your child to puzzles that contain just a few pieces. First puzzles are likely to require placing individual shapes rather than interlocking pieces. The board might have cutouts of a square, triangle, and circle. Your child fits the appropriate piece into the hole. As you participate in the game, use the words for the shapes: "Where does the triangle belong?" "Let's fit the circle here." Trial and error teaches your child he can't fit a square peg into a round hole.

When he masters this type, let him try his hand at puzzles with a picture. The picture should be very simple, however, and, if possible, the pieces should contain whole segments of the object. Help your child arrange the pieces and tell him the words for each part he's handling: "Put the dog's head here." "The feet belong here." Teach him the concepts contained in such remarks as: "too big," "turn it around," "upside down," and "all finished." Your child will enjoy putting together his puzzles over and over again and learning new language at the same time. Eventually, he'll know the puzzles well enough to do them by himself.

*Draw-a-Figure

Draw an outline of a figure on a large sheet of paper. With different-colored crayons, then draw each feature, and tell your child what you're doing: "Here is the mouth." "Here is the arm." When the figure is finished, ask him to point to each part as you name it. Then, reverse the process and ask him to tell you the name when you indicate the part. In this way, the words for the parts of your child's body become more concrete to him.

*Toys That Can Be Joined

The more your child's manual dexterity increases, the more pleasure he takes in playing with toys he can join and pull apart. There are many commercial toys such as plastic beads, discs, boxes, and rings that can be used to make a necklace, build a tower, or create a random design. As you and your child play with these toys, use the words to describe what you're doing: "put together," "pull apart," "on top of," "next to," "long piece," and "a red piece." Use language as much as possible to help your child learn new concepts while he's having fun.

5.

Up, Up, and Away: Eighteen Months to Two Years

A toddler's exuberance is an awesome thing to behold. He seems to be constantly on the go. When you take him for a walk, he races ahead to investigate whatever catches his fancy—building entrances, store windows, hot dog stands, street excavations. At home, he penetrates every nook and cranny. His energy and curiosity seem inexhaustible. As he navigates with a new degree of confidence, he's less likely to collide with your curio-laden table or to trip over a forgotten stool.

As your eighteen-month-old develops better control of his muscles, activities such as block building and coloring now galvanize his interest. He may diligently pile several blocks on top of each other, only to topple the tower in a sudden outburst of energy. A few lines on his scratch pad soon evolve into large scribbles. He develops a passion for pull-toys, and may insist on lugging a favorite stuffed animal or toy truck on his excursions into the world.

At the same time, the muscle control required for speech is also developing apace. As he is able to make more complicated muscular adjustments within his mouth, his words become more intelligible. His voice still shifts unpredictably from loud to muted, high-pitched to whisper-low, grating to smooth. He needs time to develop the physical ability to modulate his voice. It's only when he's a bit older that your child will learn to speak softly while his father is poring over the sports pages and to raise his voice in a bustling supermarket. Your own model, of course, will help him to become more skilled in controlling his voice. During this stage, your child is learning basic language skills, but he's also growing in other ways; your wisdom and sensitivity can make this an exciting, productive time for the entire family.

Growth of Awareness: A Spur to Language

Now that he walks and is learning to talk, your eighteen-month-old is alert to sights, sounds, and situations that once escaped his notice. He's fascinated now by the neighbors' dogs, pauses in rapt attention to observe the painters on their scaffold, and when you pass a fruit stand, is apt to say "apple" or "peach." New sights, new sounds, even strange smells stimulate his burgeoning interest in life.

An eighteen-month-old also perceives his own role as a separate entity within his environment. His motor and intellectual capabilities enable him to distinguish *himself* clearly from the objects and people around him. Members of his immediate household occupy a constant place in his life, but a loving grandparent or a favorite aunt is also singled out as someone "special." He recognizes those neighbors he frequently sees, as well as his playground friends. Gradually, as this consciousness of others increases, his view of the world becomes less self-centered. This growing awareness in turn serves him as a motivating force in learning the skills that other people already seem to possess, particularly the knack of talking. When your eighteen-month-old mimics your actions, he's "trying on" your behavior. When he pretends to be talking on the telephone, sweeping up the floor, or caring for a baby, he's learning to put himself in your place, to become more like you. With maturity, this natural imitation of adult behavior will affect other areas of his life—his social relationships, his attitude toward learning, and the language he uses.

An eighteen-month-old lives in the here and now. He doesn't yet have a clear concept of what happened yesterday, or what may be planned for tomorrow. When you talk with him about the events in his day you're helping him understand that there is indeed a past and a future, as well as a present.

Be sure to inform him in advance of upcoming events: "Aunt Ruth is coming to our house for lunch. She is bringing cousin Neil. Neil and you can play while Aunt Ruth and I talk in the living room. After lunch, we'll all go to the playground."

During the visit, do involve your child in the happenings: "Take Neil to your room. Show him your new tow truck." "It's time now for lunch." "Put on your green jacket, we're going to the playground now."

At the end of your day, a résumé of the day's activities is useful and will help your child remember the highlights: "Wasn't it fun having Aunt Ruth and Neil to lunch?" "Were you cold in the playground?" "What was it Neil put into your wagon?" This "discussion session" will help your toddler feel that he's actively involved in your plans and make him aware of the continuity in his life.

The limited language ability of an eighteen-month-old makes it difficult for him to tell you what he has on his mind. Nor does he have the patience of a saint; so it's tough on him to be kept waiting, and he's seldom ready to accept the grim fact that he can't always have his own way. Small wonder that children this age are infamous for their temper tantrums and eruptions of tempestuous behavior.

Kevin was contentedly soaking in his bathtub, maneuvering his flotilla in a haphazard design for naval battle, when his mother arrived to tell him it was time to return to dry land. If he didn't hurry to dress at once, he would be late for Joan's birthday party, she explained. The little admiral was unable to tell his mother just how unwelcome that news was; he was having such a smashing time, splashing about and making waves for his toy boats. The only protest he was able to mount was a curdling scream, followed by deep sobs. Notwithstanding, his bath came to an abrupt end when his mother lifted him, protesting, from the tub and wrapped him in a towel.

As Kevin's language ability increases, scenarios like this will be less emotional, if only because he'll be able to use the power of persuasion to gain a few more minutes in the tub—while his mother may use the power of reason to convince him that he must also tend to his social engagements.

Until a child learns that language can be the most effective way of winning an argument, he may react by bellowing, like Kevin, when he doesn't get his way. Or he may even react physically. When parents, in turn, respond with physical discipline, an unhappy pattern is established. Using language instead, even at this early age, teaches your child the wisdom of a more rational way of responding. As you talk to your child, you show him how language can be used to cope with life's frustrations. Sometimes, a calm and logical explanation can even get a balky child to change his mind Reason will out, if he senses that you're at least willing to consider his wishes.

Leslie was all atwitter when she heard the familiar tinkling of the ice cream truck's bell. As the truck pulled up to the curb, she tugged at her mother's hand and said, "I ceem! I ceem!" But Leslie's mother reminded her, "It's time for lunch now, you can't have any ice cream," and continued walking. Leslie began to cry and pull back toward the treat-laden truck. Her mother patiently explained that ice cream now would spoil her appetite. "But," she promised, "I'll buy you some ice cream for dessert." Leslie's sobbing abated, and she accepted her mother's compromise. The solution brought a far happier response than would have been obtained by an unequivocal "No!"

How Playmates Encourage Language

Your toddler's curiosity is now aroused when he sees other children on the street or at the playground. He looks inquisitively in their direction, and sometimes initiates contact. He may sit down quietly beside another child, or touch him, or even suddenly snatch his toy away. Although an eighteen-month-old may not yet play directly with his peers, playmates are beginning to fill an essential role in his life.

Dean is immersed in his puzzle, while Jason is absorbed with his building blocks. Although they're playing with little interaction, each is well aware of the presence of a friend. When Jason leaves the room, Dean is conscious of his absence. This period is a transition stage between the totally self-centered baby and the older, more sensitive child. Later, a child will learn to play with his friend in a spirit of give-and-take, though the participation in parallel activities still will occur from time to time. Even adults enjoy pursuing separate interests in the same room while sharing each other's companionship. You may be reading a magazine and your husband answering a letter, but each of you feels the closeness of the other.

Playing with friends helps a child learn new language while teaching him how to get along with others. In his contacts with other children, he's exposed to new words and concepts: "You can ride on Billy's rocking horse." "If it's warm enough, you can go in Darcy's wading pool." "We must see Linda's new tropical fish tank."

Although there's little or no conversation between children at this age, words occasionally tumble forth out of sheer necessity. Often a child will blurt out "Mine!" to claim dominion over some disputed toy. "My pail!" "My cup!" your child may feel compelled to explain to some visiting playmate with covetous ways. That sort of possessiveness isn't uncommon, incidentally, within this age group. It may make a child reluctant to share with his friends, but it doesn't indicate that he has a stingy soul or antisocial tendencies. Rather, it's his way of establishing the boundaries of his developing personality. "I am me," he's beginning to comprehend—and, by the same token, "This is mine."

The desirability of sharing is a feeling that will develop naturally at a somewhat later stage; for now, his language ability is apt to be too limited to let him understand the advantages of generosity.

Communicating Through Action

Physical actions continue to serve as a substitute for words for an eighteen-month-old. Nonverbal communication reflects his more highly developed physical skills, such as his increased mobility and his improved motor control. A ten-month-old baby shakes his head or pushes something aside to indicate "No." At eighteen months, he can be considerably more demonstrative. He can scurry into the living room and hide behind the couch if he decides he isn't ready for his nap.

As your child's language ability improves, his reliance on such physical actions for communication begins to diminish. Nonverbal communication never really disappears; even as adults we continue to transmit messages, on occasion, without uttering a word—deliberately at times, unconsciously at others. The way we position and move our bodies can convey a great deal to our audience, sometimes even contradicting the words we use.

Nonverbal actions in young children often express feelings they can't yet articulate. Kisses and hugs naturally say, "I love you!" Flailing fists indicate only too clearly, "I'm angry. I want that toy back." If your child hides behind Mommy's skirts or snuggles in Daddy's lap, begin to offer him the language to *verbalize* the feelings such actions communicate. "It's so nice when you hug me," he should hear you say. Or; "I love you, too." Or, again, "I know you feel shy. Sometimes I also feel shy."

While some nonverbal communication is desirable, you'll want to replace other forms—kicking, biting, and punching, for example—with words at the earliest possible moment. Unfortunately, learning to use language in place of aggressive physical behavior may require some time—and, on your part, much patience.

Your Child's Expanding Vocabulary

When you take your toddler on an escalator for the first
time, you are almost certain to use words he already
understands, such as "moving," "up," "down," and
"stairs," to describe the experience. But that's no excuse
for calling an escalator "moving stairs." Referring to this
new vehicle that your child is joyously discovering by its
rightful name will help him add to his vocabulary. You
may think it's a difficult word for him to acquire—and he
certainly isn't ready to pronounce it correctly—but he
can learn to understand it, especially since he associates
it with the day's thrilling event. Words tend to become
part of your child's little lexicon when they're repeated
and explained during direct experience, and later reinforced by repetition. Everyday situations, as well as novel
experiences, offer opportunities for acquiring new
words. Words such as "traffic" or "crosswalk" can be
taught, by use and repetition, as you promenade along
the streets. Robbie's family lives near the water, so his
parents' warning, "Don't go near the water," taught
Robbie to caution all visitors, "No dock!"

Your child's curiosity also serves to accelerate his vocabulary development. When confronted by an unfamiliar object, he may begin to pose questions, albeit in very
simple form at this stage. Pointing at your typewriter,
and saying "That?" is his way of asking, "What is that
strange instrument that makes a funny clatter sometimes?" Answer his question directly, organizing your
reply so that the word your child is seeking doesn't get
buried in a complex answer. "That is a typewriter," you
might explain. "I use it to type letters."

Don't forget to reinforce the new word in your child's
vocabulary by using it again. "I'll show you how I use my
typewriter," you should say, before beginning a brief

demonstration. Explaining "typewriter" to your child while at the same time showing him how it works helps crystallize the word in his mind, helps make language real. Never neglect an opportunity to associate new words with concrete experiences.

Most language stimulation by parents at this age consists of naming things; there's so much a child needs to identify in his environment! But you shouldn't confine your instruction to nouns alone. If you say, "Look at the dog," rather than the single word "dog," this encourages your child to use sentences. When he has mastered the mental and physical gymnastics required to say words consecutively, he might begin by repeating, "Look, dog!" Two- or three-word phrases mark the beginning of your child's ability to use connected speech. "Up!" soon is expanded to "Pick up!" "Push" may now be expressed as "Push swing!" "Give," clarified, becomes "Give me ball!" The flowering of words into such simple phrases indicates that your child is learning how to organize and express his thoughts more completely.

How Listening Skills Help Vocabulary Growth

The sounds in your child's environment are a growing source of interest to him at this stage. He learns to distinguish among various sounds and to react appropriately. He can now identify the sound of the lawn mower and quickly recognize a fire engine's siren. The ability to make such gross sound discriminations helps a child appreciate the subtler differences between speech sounds. Speaking and understanding language requires the ability to recognize the unique combinations of sounds that make words. By identifying the sounds in his environ-

ment, you're helping your child isolate them, helping
him to develop his auditory awareness.

Now that your toddler's listening ability is stretching,
he's able to follow basic directions: "Put the blocks on
the shelf." "Give me your dish." "Bring me your shoes."
Letting him perform simple errands makes your child
feel grown-up and encourages him to listen more attentively. Clarify your requests by also employing some
physical directions, if necessary.

Jill's mother asked her to fetch the sweater that was
draped over a chair across the room. When Jill appeared
to be confused, her mother pointed her in the right direction, then repeated her request. Letting your child
help you with some household chores, provided the du-
ties you assign him are simple enough, will help him gain
a feeling of competency and help expand his auditory
memory.

Language Learning Takes Time

Should you be alarmed if your child isn't speaking at all?
The answer to that question is really a series of additional questions. Is your child developing normally in
other ways? Does he seem to understand you when you
speak to him? Does his hearing appear to be normal? Is
there any special event in your child's life that could
account for the delay? Is there any situation in your
home that may be troubling your child?

Your responses can help identify a physical or emotional problem that may be interfering with your child's
language learning. The earlier a problem is recognized,
the more effectively it can be dealt with. But remember,
too, that some children, though they may be perfectly
healthy, mentally sound, and emotionally well balanced,
don't begin to speak until after the age of two, and

thereafter do develop normal language. Remember, too, that there are wide individual differences in the rates at which children learn to speak. Some start quite early and continue adding to their vocabularies; others seem to require more time to "case" life's perplexities. Still other children may start talking at a very early age, only to reach a plateau at which little further growth seems to occur.

Just because your child has developed a rudimentary vocabulary, don't expect him to repeat every new word you want to teach him. You may provide the necessary information and experiences, you may even stimulate conversation, but it's up to your child to decide what to say and when to say it. Badgering your eighteen-month-old with nagging demands such as "Say ball," or "Say doggie," can hinder his speech development. Constant pressures can cause some children to tune out and turn off. In such circumstances, children may withhold speech purposely to defeat crusading parents. It's their way of saying, "Lay off, already!" The fact is, a child begins using words when he's ready. Giving your child the necessary stimulation in an encouraging atmosphere can help him to be ready sooner than prodding and carping.

At no time should you attempt to correct your child's way of saying words; your corrections only confuse him. As he gains greater facility in making sounds and a more discriminating auditory sense, he'll correct himself. Allow your child to learn language at his own pace and in his own manner. Pressure, no matter how well intended, will only disturb the learning process.

Language: An Invaluable Tool

A child doesn't learn to speak merely to please his Mommy and Daddy. There has to be a more compelling motivation: the need for a tool that will help him satisfy his wants, earn him recognition, persuade others, and get people to respond to him. When your child, on impulse, decides he'd rather push the stroller than ride in it, let him have his way if that's at all possible. Your trip home may be longer and more onerous as a result, but you'll be letting your youngster know that his words exert influence over you. Take advantage of whatever situations arise during the day that may let you reinforce the values of language. Convince him that language can really "put him in touch" with you and with others.

The positive response your child receives from others teaches him the value of language as a social instrument. When Grandma rewards his use of "please" (though it be pronounced "pease") and "thanks" (though it comes out sounding more like "tantoo") by offering him another cookie, you can well imagine what assets these words become to him. Like money in the bank!

As you read the following section, keep in mind that some eighteen-month-olds are already speaking in short sentences, while others have yet to say their first word. Adapt the activities to your own child's language capabilities—and do encourage all his efforts. Don't allow yourself or your child to become frustrated by some word game that's clearly unsuited to his level of competence. Learning language should be fun, not a grueling chore. The more your toddler relishes language, the sooner he's motivated to use it, and the more proficient he'll become.

ACTIVITIES

Learning Speech Sounds

Much of the stimulation you've provided up to now has been directed at building receptive language. Your input has given your child the foundation he needs to say words. Now that he has begun to speak, you can help him learn to say speech sounds properly by having fun with these sounds in speech games. As he listens to you produce the sounds and watches the movements of your mouth, he learns the correct way of saying them. Your speech model and the extra stimulation you can provide help him modify his way of speaking.

The activities described in this section are designed to heighten your toddler's awareness of individual sounds and should never be used to criticize or correct his speech. At this age, he's still in a formative stage and most of the sounds he produces won't be perfected for some time. Accept and copiously praise all his speech efforts. Gradually, his production of speech sounds will become more accurate. Your goal at this stage is to intensify the stimulation your child is receiving from the normal flow of conversation. Although begun at this age, these speech-sound activities should be continued for years to come. Start developing the resources described in the activities now and add to them as your child becomes able to handle more complex material.

Sound Names make individual speech sounds more concrete for your child. Develop names for different speech sounds, and associate these names with something in your child's environment or experience: *s*—the snake sound; *m*—the humming top sound; *ch*—the choo-choo train sound; *t*—the tick-tock sound; *z*—buzzing fly sound; *p*—popcorn sound; *r*—the growl of a dog. Use these sound names when you play with the objects, and let your child hear you make the sound: Move his toy snake along the floor and make the hissing *s* sound. As his top spins, hum the *m* sound. Accompany the ticking of his toy clock with your own *t-t-t.* Make believe you're a fly buzzing *z-z-z* your way around the room. Make a train with your child: Hold him around the waist and pretend he's the engine as you repeat the *ch* sound. Pretend you're both dogs and growl the sound *r.* Make popcorn and while listening to it pop, say *p.*

Use your imagination to create names for other speech sounds. Any sound name referring to something special in your child's experience will make the sound even more meaningful. As he becomes familiar with these sound games, he may repeat the sounds with you. If not, just hearing the sounds from you provides him with valuable auditory experiences.

Sound Poems. By letting your child hear nursery rhymes, other poems, or songs that use a certain sound repeatedly, you reinforce the correct production of the speech sound. For example, "Ba Ba Black Sheep" highlights the sound *b,* "Jack and Jill" repeats the sound *j,* "To Market, to Market" uses the sound *m* frequently, "Peter, Peter, Pumpkin Eater" includes the *p* sound often, and in "Simple Simon" the *s* is emphasized.

Use your child's collections of poetry to find other suitable material. Don't emphasize the sound unnaturally when you say the poem. Let your child hear you say the words normally. But you can use any special actions that would make the poems more fun. "Clocks" offers many opportunities for your child to hear the sound *t* and the words themselves might very well be accompanied by body actions:

Slowly ticks the big clock:
Tick-tock, tick-tock!
But Cuckoo clock ticks double quick:
Tick-a-tock-a, tick-a-tock-a,
Tick-a-tock-a, tick!

Sound Box. Collect small objects that all begin with the same sound, and place them in boxes, letting each box hold only objects beginning with the same sound. In the *l* box, you might have a leaf, lipstick, a toy lamp, a piece of lace, and a miniature lamb and lion. The *p* box could include a penny, a pencil, a piece of paper, a toy pig, paints, a pen, and a miniature pot. For the *d* box you might assemble a dish, a doll, a toy duck and dog, a dime, and a doll's dress. To stimulate language, talk about the objects of one box at a time; this provides your child with ample practice of each sound: "Here's a new penny." "Can you write with the pencil?" "Give your doll some food on the dish."

Picture File. Gather pictures for each sound from magazines, catalogs, newspapers, or your own drawings, and paste them on paper or cardboard. Let your child help you select the pictures to be included for each sound. Talking about the pictures reinforces the correct production of the sound, increases your child's vocabulary, and teaches him new facts.

Picture Stories. Make up simple stories about each picture in your file. For a picture of a tractor, you might say: "This is a tractor. The farmer uses the tractor on his farm. He drives it in the field. The tractor is yellow." When your child develops enough language, ask *him* to tell you a story about one of the pictures.

Fishing Game. Put paper clips on several small pictures for a particular sound from your picture file. Then let your child "fish" them up from the floor or a table with a magnet attached to a string. Tell him the name of each picture and have him repeat it as he hauls in his catch. When he's familiar with the pictures, let him say the words without any help.

Creating Playthings for Language Learning

Objects in the home can be used for language learning in limitless ways. Before you discard empty egg cartons, milk containers, cereal boxes, other cardboard cartons, boxes with dividers, styrofoam molds, jar lids, wooden spools, plastic meat trays from the supermarket, plastic bottles, and paper-towel tubes, examine them for their play and language-learning possibilities (assuming they're clean and don't contain potential hazards).

Boxes. Large and small cartons attract most children. If they're big enough, you child enjoys climbing in and out of them. Make language part of his play: "Where shall the doll sleep?" "Let's pretend this box is a fire engine." Smaller boxes can become "sound boxes" as well as storage places for your child's treasures or for toys with many pieces. He'll love emptying them out, and now is the time to start encouraging him to put the pieces back in the box as well. Talk about the objects he puts away: "This fits here." "That's too big for this box." Boxes with a long string attached become wonderful pull toys. Shoe boxes are ideal for giving dolls a ride. Talk about which doll he'll take and where they're going.

Containers. Put some pebbles in a plastic container and seal the lid to make a rhythm instrument. Show your child how to shake the container as he sings and dances. You might also improvise a drum from a can that has a lid and beat out a rhythm. Plastic bottles and jars with screw-on tops are also appealing. Children learn to turn the top to "put the lid on" and "take it off." They enjoy filling a container with water or sand and then emptying it. Use language to describe your child's actions: "Fill the bottle." "Pour it out." "Put the cap on." "Turn the lid."

Paper Bags. Shopping bags and other paper bags of all shapes and sizes stimulate creative play and language. Your child may discover his own original way of using a paper bag. Offer suggestions: "Let's make a hat with this bag," or, "Stuff this bag with old socks and we'll make a ball."

Homemade Dolls. Dolls you make at home to represent members of your family are more meaningful than those that depict comic book characters or people from a popular television show. Use them to elicit language as you act out situations from your child's daily life: "Daddy is ringing the doorbell." "Here's Mommy taking care of the baby." The process of creating the dolls is a valuable language experience, since you and your child can discuss such considerations as "how big," "what color," "which shape," and "how many." Allow him to help as much as possible. At this age, he might be able to hand you the fabric or the thread. When he's older, he might like to try his hand at painting or sewing.

How to Use the Telephone

Your child is fascinated by the telephone and aware of its "magical powers." It rings and people's voices come out of one end; you can even talk to them! At this age, your child may demand his turn to talk on the telephone. Even though he's very insistent, he may just stare at the receiver dumbfounded when you hand it to him. Encourage him to talk into the telephone; tell him what to say if he has trouble getting started. Toy telephones are wonderful for imaginary chats. You can pretend to be Daddy calling from the office: "Hello, this is Daddy. Is Philip home?" At first, you'll do most of the talking. When your child becomes accustomed to the telephone and develops sufficient language, he'll participate in the conversation.

The telephone can also be a device to help you handle unacceptable behavior: "Hello, is this Heather? Please stop banging your hammer on the window. I'm afraid the window will break. Goodbye." Heather may be more receptive to this approach than to conventional methods of discipline.

Children enjoy toy telephones for some time. As they begin to interact with their friends, they use the telephone for conversations. When your child gets older, you'll discard many of his infant toys, but don't give away the telephone too quickly. He'll find new ways of using it as his language develops.

Spatial Relations

Use your child's toys to develop the language for size, shape, and space discrimination. Although his vocabulary for these concepts is quite small and his comprehension somewhat vague, you can strengthen his understanding through the language you use: "This truck is little." "Bring me that heavy car." "Where is your big box?" "Feel how light this doll is."

Puzzles develop an awareness of shapes and the way different ones can be related. Many children at this age can complete a puzzle with several pieces. Finding the location of the pieces provides many opportunities for language: "This piece goes near the top." "Put it next to the round one." Other toys increase your child's understanding of how objects relate to each other and move in space. The fire engine can go fast, slow, forward, and backward. The book can be open, closed, under or on top of the table. The doll's dress can be on, off, buttoned, or unbuttoned. Use language to accompany your child's play. As he listens to words in the context of his activity, he learns their meaning through concrete demonstrations.

Listening for Information

Fetch and Carry teaches your child to listen to instructions. Show your child two items and place them in the room. Ask him to bring you the objects one at a time: "Bring me the towel"; then, "Bring me the bowl." When he's able to complete this task successfully, vary the game by asking him to bring you objects without showing them to him first. Choose a room where he knows the location of most things. In his own room, ask him to bring you some of his toys: "Bring me your ball." "Bring me your music box." "Bring me your book." After you have a collection in your lap, reverse the process: "Put away your ball." Then, when the ball is back on the shelf, say, "Put away your music box," and then, "Put away your book." He must select the correct item and return it to its proper place. As you can see, this game has more than one benefit.

Listening to Stories

The times you and your child spend with a book are among some of the most enriching moments. "Story hour" is a good opportunity for physical closeness as well as language learning. Now that your child is more independent and on the go all the time, your chances to sit and hold him on your lap are fewer and fewer. If he doesn't seem to be in the mood to sit still, however, postpone the story. Bedtime is the traditional occasion for story telling, but you need not limit yourself to it. Perhaps your child's more interested in a story after lunch, or when you come home from the playground, or after his nap.

If the text in a book is too complicated, tell your own version of the story or use the illustrations as inspiration for a totally new story. Include some of the people, pets, objects, or events in your child's life in your story. You may surprise yourself with your talent at this kind of improvisation.

When you read to your child, make him an active participant. Have him identify pictures either verbally, by asking, "What is that?" or physically, by saying, "Show me the ———." Ask his opinion about the characters or the action: "Where did Jack and Jill go?" or "What did the Mommy bird feed her children?" Soon, he may "help" you tell the story. If his attention wanders, these departures from the story itself can help him concentrate again. Stop when you feel your child has had enough; it's always better to end an activity before your child tires of it. Here's a list of some books a child this age will enjoy:

Baby's First Counting Book. New York: Platt & Munk Publishers.

Jean Bethell, *The Touch and Tell Book.* New York: Grosset & Dunlap, 1976.

Hilde Heyduck Huth, *In the Village.* New York: Harcourt, Brace & World, 1968.

Ruthanna Long, *10 Little Chipmunks.* New York: Golden Press, 1974.

Kent Salisbury, *Funny Fingers*. New York: Golden
Press, 1971.
Richard Scarry, *Egg in the Hole Book*. New York:
Golden Press, 1976.

How to Teach Discrimination Between Sounds

The following activities help your child learn to differentiate between sounds in his environment. With practice,
he'll learn to make the necessary discriminations between speech sounds. Some of these speech sounds—*s*
and *l*, for example—are quite different; others, like *t* and
d are more similar and, therefore, require finer auditory
discrimination. In order to understand words—and then
to speak—a child must learn to hear the differences between speech sounds.

Sounds Around Us teaches your child to recognize the
source of the sounds in his environment. Identify the
distinctive noises in your home and outside as well. Tell
him the names of the objects and repeat the sounds they
make: "The siren on the fire engine says, 'Ah-ah-ah-
ah.'" "The train says, 'Choo-choo.'" "The bell says,
'ding dong.'" Encourage your child to imitate the
sounds with you. Draw his attention to sounds he may
not notice: "Listen to that loud noise outside. What do
you think made that sound? Is it a fire engine or a gar-
bage truck? Let's look and see."

Let's Make the Sound teaches your child to differentiate
between the sounds objects make and to learn their
names. Assemble two or three objects such as keys, a
little bell, or a noisemaker. Place the objects on a table
in front of your child and make the sound of each object
as you say its name. Next, show him how to make the
sound. Repeat the name of the object when he produces

the sound, and ask him to say the word when you make the sound.

Show Me the _____ helps your child learn to listen for meaning. Place two objects on a table. Tell him the name of each one and let him say the words with you. After you're sure he knows the name of each object, ask him to point to the one you name. Say, "Show me the crayon," and see if he can respond correctly. If he has difficulty, point to the object and repeat its name. Add to the number of items he must identify as he becomes more familiar with the game and learns the names of more objects.

ADVANCED ACTIVITIES

*Concentration

Place two objects from one of the sound boxes on a table. Ask your child to name each one. Then tell him to turn around and when he does, remove one of the objects. He must guess which object is missing. When he's able to play "concentration" easily, increase the number of objects he must remember.

*Treasure Hunt

Hide a few objects from a sound box rather conspicuously in a room. Tell your child the names of the objects you've hidden and ask him to find them. As he brings each one to you, have him repeat the name of the object.

Choose one sound box at a time for this activity. Then, you might try hiding the objects without first telling your toddler which ones he's looking for. Each time he finds one, tell him how many are left. Your child might enjoy hiding the objects for you to find when he's a bit older.

*Picture Concentration

Play a concentration game with the pictures from your picture file. Place two pictures on a table and ask your child to name each one. Then turn both pictures face down and ask your child to turn over the one you name and repeat the word. As his skill increases, add to the pictures he must remember. Let him ask you to turn over a specific picture when he gains more confidence in playing the game.

6.
The Terrific Twos: Two to Three Years

By the time you place two glistening candles on his birthday cake, your child will probably be tossing off words and even using a few simple phrases. Though he won't be holding press conferences for some time yet, the next year should see an astonishing growth in his use of language. By his third birthday, his vocabulary will have made great strides and he should be piecing together longer and more complex sentences. During this second year, your child really begins to assert himself and he'll be playing a greater role in managing his life. He may begin to choose his own clothing, and the kinds of foods, fun, and frolic that give him the most pleasure. "By golly, I'm me," he seems to be saying. "I'm my own person. And I think I can do it myself."

A two-year-old's self-discovery will be reflected in a new degree of confidence, and a willingness to test his physical mettle. Your erstwhile toddler no longer toddles about on wobbly underpinnings. His legs have grown sturdy and steady; he relies on them to walk properly, to run, leap, and jump. He'll be showing off on the monkey bars and cannonballing down the playground slide with squeals of pride. Racing about on his new tricycle, he may seem bent on breaking the town ordinances. When will they install traffic lights for wee speed-demons?

At this stage, your "do-it-myself" child can help take some of the drudgery out of your day. Mealtimes should become less hectic now that he's becoming adept at feeding himself. While you scour the tub for his bath, he begins to undress himself. At bedtime, he starts to climb, mostly unaided, into his pajamas. The years of cribs and bibs, prams and high chairs, bottles and formulas, diapers and rattles are nearing their end. Babyhood is giving ground to childhood.

How Vocabulary Grows

Between the ages of two and three, your child's vocabulary triples. He'll be chattering about things that interest him and also trying to master the words he hears used by members of the family. He'll even be attempting tricky jargon like "helicopter" and "missiles." A child's lexicon reflects his parents' hobbies: Since Paul's parents are avid sailors, words like "mast" and "rudder," "fore" and "aft" became part of his earliest vocabulary, just as an orange life jacket was one of his first outer garments.

Many children are introduced to toilet training during this year, and it is also a time when they begin to learn the differences between the sexes. Reproduction is probably not uppermost in a two-year-old's mind, but he's definitely tuned into what boys have and what girls have, as well as what mommies and daddies have. This budding sexual awareness is intensified as a child focuses on the sensations associated with controlling his own body functions. Discussions about sexual organs, as they relate to toilet training, form the basis for later exchanges of information about more mature sex topics.

Your honesty—or dishonesty—influences both the content and language of these discussions. Myths surrounding toilet habits, like those about where babies come from, though convenient for a time, eventually have to be unlearned. Your clear explanations now can make the process go more smoothly in other areas when he's older. The words you use to describe body functions and sexual organs should be language you feel comfortable with. At this age, it doesn't matter whether your child hears clinical language or your own pet expressions. Just be sure these pet expressions don't have any double meanings that could cause confusion. Teaching a little boy to call his penis his "pee pee" might create a misunderstanding when his friend's mother asks him if he wants to "make pee pee." Your two-year-old should be acquainted with commonly used terms as well as with your own "cute" expressions. He should understand "penis" and "vagina" even though you've taught him to say, "peter" and "penie" or "vee vee" and "viney." So familiarize him with the "real" words now that he'll be spending more and more time with others. Using words you feel comfortable with communicates your relaxed attitude and helps eliminate the sense of taboo often associated with these subjects.

What you may consider private body functions are public to a child this age. On a crowded bus, your toilet-trained two-year-old may announce loudly and clearly exactly what he has "to do." If "I have to make a doody!" would embarrass you, perhaps you should also teach him the less specific "I have to go to the bathroom." Your future ability to confidently discuss such potentially sensitive issues as masturbation, sexual relations, homosexuality, and reproduction begins with your frank approach to toilet training.

While becoming more aware of his body, your child also develops an interest in his vital statistics. He learns his precise age, attempts to pronounce his last name, and remembers the address of his house or apartment. Such newly acquired data represent one more step in your child's ability to use language to express his understanding of himself and his environment.

Children are natural mimics who tend to sop up with little discrimination everything they hear. If certain words offend you, you had best guard against their inadvertent use in your child's presence. If, as is likely in today's permissive society, he picks up undesirable words despite your best efforts, the most effective remedy is to ignore their use. Drawing attention to some vulgarism only makes its use more attractive. We're all familiar with the rebel gleam that lights up a child's eye when he utters some forbidden word or phrase. These words should lose their glamour and fade away to their proper place in his memory bank if you turn a deaf ear to them.

As your child's vocabulary grows, he begins to join words to make short sentences. The child who once demanded, "Cookie!" while pointing toward the kitchen larder may soon be saying, "Me want cookie!" Although giving your child a cookie when he asks for it reinforces his use of language as a way to get what he wants, if it's not snack time, watch out! He now has the language to try to move you from your resolve not to give him anything just before a meal. He may insist, somewhat petulantly: "In the cabinet." Stick to your guns, though, or very soon he'll realize he can "con" you with words.

At this age children can start combining several sentences about the same subject. After a trip to the aquar-

ium with her father, Francine breathlessly informed her
mother about the day's experiences in a tumble of sentences that touched on the dolphin's tricks, the antics of
the baby whale, the ice cream treat, and the bus ride
home. The interest Francine's mother communicated
through her comments and questions showed Francine
that she had something worthwhile to say. Francine's
confidence in her ability to hold a real conversation
grew, and she was motivated to use connected language
in order to tell her mother about other exciting adventures.

Learning Sounds Takes Time

Again, the most effective way to help your child's speech
development is to present a good model. When, in his
own fashion, he says "wape up" for "wake up" or
"puddy" for "pillow," don't draw these flaws to his attention. And above all, don't imitate them. Eventually,
he'll learn the right way to say these words by listening
to you tell him, "It's time to wake up" or "Here's your
pillow."

Two-year-olds tend to substitute certain sounds for
others. Often they interchange the *th* for *s* as in "thoap"
for "soap"; the *w* for *r* as in "wed" for "red"; or the *y*
for *l* as in "yike" for "like." Parents must avoid reinforc-
ing these sound substitutions by repeating them. Sara
may sound quite fetching proclaiming, "My name is
Thara," and Donny may be irresistible when he avows,
"I love my wabbit," but what strikes a parent as adorable
in a two-year-old shouldn't be reinforced by smiles or
any other signs of parental approval. For if Sara hears
herself called "Thara" often enough, she might come to
regard it as her rightful name. And Donny might still be

saying "wabbits" way beyond the age when it's considered cute.

On the other hand, don't insist that your child repeat each word correctly. At this point in life, he may not be able to make the precise sound that's required. Instead, you might reply, "Yes, your name is Sara," or "Your rabbit is on your bed." What's essential, we must repeat, is that your child hear your own correct speech. When he's ready and able, he'll shed the baby talk.

Not uncommonly, you may find your child using a word or two, or even a sentence, that's completely unintelligible to you. This makes for a frustrating communication gap, to put it mildly. If your child repeats himself but you still can't decipher his meaning, try to elicit some more clues: "Show me what you want. Is it something to eat? Is it something to play with? Is it something in this room?" If your best efforts fail, try to distract him for the moment. Later, he may find a different, more effective way of communicating his idea.

"Why? Why? Why?"

As your child's abilities to express his boundless curiosity develop, you may find yourself becoming a full-time, unpaid Answer Man (or Woman). He wants to know the names of people and objects, and why people and things behave as they do. Everything is reduced to whys, and your answers seem only to generate more whys. The child appears to be insatiable. And sometimes your answers sound unconvincing. (Well, why *is* "up" in that direction? And why is "down" in the other?) Once your inquisitor has run through his repertoire of questions, he may begin to ask the same ones again.

Little Laura's dinner conversation keeps her family

forever on their toes. "Why are the string beans green?" she asks. "Because there's a chemical in them, called chlorophyll, that makes them green," her mother answers. "Why are they called string beans?" "Because there are stringy fibers on the pod," her father replies between mouthfuls. And "Why do farmers grow them?" "Because they're good for people to eat," her brother contributes. Why and why—from the soup course to the rice pudding. Laura's parents would require a refresher course in general science and some boning up on food production statistics to keep abreast of their daughter's curiosity. The simple answers Laura's family provides satisfy her probing. Wisely, they don't overwhelm her with excessive details.

Try to be patient when your child poses a maddening series of endless questions. If you're busy, ask him to wait until you can give his inquiries your full attention, but do furnish the answers as soon as you have a free moment, using simple language he can understand. Remember, your child isn't only eager for information, he's also flexing his language muscles through these questions, and not deliberately subjecting you to torture. He's trying to solve some of the mysteries of a new and puzzling world, to discover just where he fits in the dizzying scheme of things. Of course, he may also be using the questions to gain attention—to make sure he's properly recognized.

Even in the adult world, questions open the door to conversation. In striking up a new acquaintance, you may ask, "How long have you been living in this neighborhood?" or "Do you know Mrs. So-and-So?" One query leads to another, and answers establish rapport while broadening two people's pool of mutual information. So with a child, your straightforward answers allow the sharing of information. More important, they lay the foundations for more meaningful communication.

Childhood Nonfluency—A Normal Stage

Many children go through a period of nonfluency between the ages of two and four. This nonfluency may take the form of the repetition of the first sound of a word (b-b-b-baby), or of the first syllable (ba-ba-ba-baby), or again of the entire word (the-the-the-the baby is crying). Such noticeable nonfluencies are often incorrectly labeled "stuttering" or "stammering," and can cause a flurry of worry among parents agonizing as their child struggles to complete his thought.

The chances are that your child isn't upset by his hesitant speech. But if he indicates that it does trouble him, you might calm his apprehension by explaining that everyone—Mommy and Daddy too—has trouble speaking from time to time. Few of us have glib, golden tongues a hundred percent of the time. *The vast majority of children pass through this stage unaffected and then speak with normal fluency.*

There are positive steps to take during this time to help your child. Listen to him attentively and accept his efforts without interrupting. As we already indicated, you should adopt a supportive, uncritical attitude toward all his speech attempts. When your child experiences difficulty, be a sympathetic audience. You may be sorely tempted to help finish his halting sentences or even to put an end to his awkward attempts at conversation, but keep your impatience in check. Let him complete his thoughts in his own fashion and at his own revved-up or pokey pace.

Most important, don't, in any way, draw your child's attention to his nonfluencies. And try your best not to communicate your own concern to him. It may seem helpful to tell your child to slow down, take a deep breath, start over again, talk slowly, or think out his phrases before he speaks. Actually, any advice of this kind can be quite damaging. Your interference could well become a source of tension and convince your child that his speech simply doesn't measure up. And once such a notion is communicated, he may begin to feel insecure and unhappy—both about his speech and himself.

It's particularly important at this time to provide a relaxed atmosphere. Don't rush, push, or crowd your child. Allow enough time for him to get through his day with a minimum of pressure. One mother at our local playground, whose two-and-a-half-year-old son was going through a period of obvious nonfluency, was obliged to meet her older child's school bus at three o'clock each afternoon. Routinely, at two-thirty, there was a scene of screaming and caterwauling because Steven wasn't ready to take leave of his friends. Mutual anger and frustration ensued. The mother was anxious not to miss the school bus while Steven vociferously expressed his own unwillingness to get moving just yet. The pressure on the child was at last relieved when his mother realized that he merely needed more time to wind up his feverish playground activities. Now, at two o'clock each day she serves a first notice: "Steven, finish your game and pick up your toys. We have to meet Billy's bus soon." After a second reminder, and perhaps a third, it's close to two-thirty and Steven and his mother are amicably ready to start on their way home.

Whatever the nature of the conflicts between you and your child, postpone them until he passes this stage of nonfluent speech. If you find yourselves battling over eating, bedtime, toilet training, or anything else, learn to make a hasty retreat. You can always deal with those issues at a later, more appropriate, time.

Brenda and her parents were locked in a power struggle over the child's continued use of her bottle. But when

Brenda developed nonfluencies, her parents were advised to remove all pressures. They accommodated Brenda with bottle or cup, or whatever made the child feel most comfortable. Interestingly enough, as Brenda's speech gained in fluency, the "battle of the bottle," which once had loomed as a fight to the finish, resolved itself quite smoothly.

The reactions and attitudes of others are crucial in helping your child cope with nonfluencies. Members of your family, friends, baby sitters, and visiting relatives all should be made aware of how to react to his speech. They should be warned not to mimic him or to poke fun at his obvious problems. Instead, they should learn to listen patiently and avoid completing his words or sentences. Explain all of this to them—out of earshot of your child, to be sure—and add that the stage of nonfluency is a temporary one that requires an adult's forbearance.

This is not the time to push your child into the limelight, to make him the main attraction at family gatherings. Resist the temptation to get him to sing the ditty he just learned or to recite the nursery rhyme he's committed to memory. Of course, if your child volunteers to perform, accept with pleasure.

Your understanding will give your child the support he must have at this stage. It's only natural that as a parent you'll be troubled by nonfluencies. But as you become aware of what's happening to your child, and of how you can help him, your concern will diminish.

Language—The Verbal Expression of Thoughts

Words express thoughts even as thoughts form words. Your child's ability to use language with the flexibility required to express what he thinks and feels should grow by leaps and bounds this year. There are many opportunities to show your child how language can be used to think more clearly and effectively. Making choices, planning, and reasoning are all part of the growing process. You can help your toddler develop the inner language so essential to these thought processes, as well as the expressive language with which he can let the world know his conclusions.

Decisions, decisions! Painful or pleasurable, big or small, they come in all varieties. Whether we dread them, postpone them, or welcome them, one thing is sure: They're an unavoidable part of everyday life. Even your intrepid two-year-old is faced with making his own decisions. Remember that his self-confidence is given a boost whenever he can make his own free choices, whenever he realizes that his own opinions aren't without value. Choosing helps feed your child's feeling of independence.

There are many times during the day when you can encourage your child to choose between alternatives. Let him select his own lunch menu, limiting the options, perhaps, to Grilled Cheese Cordon Bleu or Chef's Deluxe Peanut Butter and Jelly Sandwich. Other opportunities abound for letting your child make his own decisions: "Do you want me to read *The Three Bears* or *Little Red Riding Hood*?" "Do you want to take your ball to the park—or your pail and shovel?" "Do you want your milk in the red glass or the blue one?"

Along with freedom to make choices, young children of this age should begin to realize the consequences of their actions. When he saw Debbie tilting her ice cream cone at a precarious angle, her father explained that the scoop would fall from the cone if she didn't hold it properly. Debbie was offered a clear choice: Continue to hold the cone at a crazy angle and risk losing her treat or straighten it and enjoy it to the last delicious dribble. Debbie's father didn't insist that she hold the cone the right way; he merely explained the reason for his suggestion. Debbie was provided with the raw material needed to make the simple decision. By using such reasoning methods, parents can avoid nagging and help their child think more constructively.

When children are allowed to participate in planning their time, they soon learn that certain events precede others. Ben and his mother were baking cookies. As Ben's mother prepared the ingredients, Ben put them into the mixing bowl. He was ready to eat the raw dough at once, but his mother explained that the batter must first be put onto a cookie sheet and then baked in the oven. Once the cookies were in the oven, Ben's mother set the timer and told Ben to listen for the bell. When he heard that alarm, Ben was again prepared to sample the cookies without further delay. Now his mother explained the cookies were too hot to eat. Ben hovered over the steaming cookies and blew on them to help them cool faster. The point is: His mother's careful use of language helped Ben understand that a sequence of events is necessary to complete such tasks as cookie baking.

Language can be consciously used as a tool to help your child plan his day and anticipate his activities: "After your nap, we'll go to the playground." "When we finish putting away your toys, I'll read you a story." "Jenny is coming over to play when we finish lunch." Of course, the best-laid plans of mothers also go awry. It may start to rain after the nap; story time may have to be postponed if the telephone rings; Jenny may develop the sneezles and have to stay in bed. Once again, language can be useful. It helps you teach your child to face such minor disappointments and to plan alternative activities: "Let's finger-paint since we can't go to the playground."

"Start looking at the pictures in your book, and I'll read the story after my phone call." "Let's call Adam and see if he can come to play, since Jenny is sick." In this way, your child begins to appreciate how language can be used to cope with problems and even to enrich his life.

How Social Experiences Help Language

Conversations with your two-year-old can be a joy. Keep your ears primed for opening gambits that will permit a nourishing exchange of ideas. Cathy was riding with her father when she noticed a truck hauling new cars. "Look at that truck, Daddy," she began. Cathy's father let this simple observation lead to more talk about the truck. "Where is it going?" Cathy wanted to know. "How did those cars get up on its back? How will they get off again?" Cathy's father patiently answered the myriad questions and carefully encouraged Cathy to articulate her curiosity. A genuinely interested parent can provide a child with the motivation for creating new language while at the same time offering a wealth of information.

Your child also adds to his vocabulary and learns new ideas through friendships. Social contacts through play groups and informal visits, in playgrounds and back yards, will occur with more and more frequency now, and an expanding circle of friends will play an important role in your child's development. He'll talk with pride at home about his friends and look forward eagerly to their visits. Playing with other children increases your child's need for self-expression. So, whenever possible, allow adequate time for your child to mingle with his peers. It doesn't just provide him with fun, it's also a valuable learning experience.

As your child grows, he spends longer periods of time at each of the activities he enjoys. This increased attention span becomes evident in his approach to his toys, his ability to listen to a story without squirming, or his willingness to master a new game without losing patience. Though you'll continue to direct many of his activities, your two-year-old, more and more, will begin to voice his own opinions. He may insist on hearing that same beloved story over and over again, though the reading of it may have started boring you to tears. Yet for a long while no other story seems to satisfy him. Then, just when you're convinced that one more repetition will make you blow your cool, he'll suddenly (we hope) choose some other favorite.

A relaxed approach to language activities on your part, and the acceptance of your child's abilities, will create an atmosphere that encourages language growth. One most valuable tool for language development is imagination— both yours and your child's. Adapt any of the language activities in the following section to your own use and create new ones. Above all, be alert to your child's ideas, even the most fanciful ones, and try to follow his suggestions whenever possible. Sometimes it is the child who leads.

ACTIVITIES

How to Achieve Self-Identification

At this age, your child becomes aware of his own individuality, while also recognizing the characteristics he shares with others. In this way, he forms a self-image that's shaped as he grows.

Language helps the two-year-old understand how the

parts of his body combine to make him a unique person.
The names of most parts of his body and some of their
functions become familiar to him: "My eyes see." "I
carry my doll in my arms." "I throw the ball with my
hand." Those features that are distinctive are also appreciated: "My eyes are blue." "I am a girl." "My hair is
very long." These observations help reinforce your
child's body concepts.

Molding Figures is a concrete way to locate and learn the
parts of the body. Using clay or play dough, help your
child form arms and legs that can be attached to a torso.
A round ball makes a head, while buttons or pebbles can
be the features and can also be used to suggest clothing.
Talk about the names and functions of the parts of the
body as you add them to the figure.

Collage Figures can be made from any materials. Draw
an outline of a figure on a large piece of paper. Paste
buttons, ribbon, string, fabric, yarn, pictures from magazines, crepe paper, tin foil, or anything else you may have
on the paper to fill in the outline. Talk about how you
might create each part of the body using different shapes
and textures: "What shall we use for the hair?" "Where
do the buttons belong?" "Would you rather use crepe
paper or fabric for the dress?"

Action Figures made from pipe cleaners or wires can
teach the language for motion as you talk about how the
body moves. The feet can be running, the arm throwing,
or the torso sitting. After your child has become familiar
with the words for different actions, position the figure
and ask him to guess what it's doing. If he's able, ask him
to position the figure and then you guess the action.

Can You Do This? encourages your child to talk about
what his body can do and helps him develop a sense of
himself in relation to space. In this activity he follows
your directions for large body movements: "Sit on the

floor." "Shake your head." "Run to the door." "Jump up and down." Allow him to give the directions as he becomes more familiar with the language needed for this game.

Learning by Listening

Your two-year-old's language growth and increased attention span are reflected in the way he begins to differentiate sounds and report what he hears. The following activities help develop the ability to interpret sounds. They also develop the language your child needs to talk about his increased auditory awareness and skill in identifying objects.

What Is It? teaches your child the difference between the sounds of various objects. Show your child two objects that make distinct sounds. Let him listen to each one. Then, make one of the sounds and ask him which object made the sound. Gradually increase the number of objects. Use anything you think might be suitable: bell, noisemaker, keys, rattling dishes, eggbeater, whistle.

Who Am I? teaches your child animal sounds. Show him two pictures or figures of animals he knows, such as a cow and a pig. Say, "Moo," and ask him to identify the correct animal. Eliminate the picture clues as his skill increases and have him guess the animals just by listening to the sound.

Loud and Soft develops your child's concept of the volume of sounds. Tell your child to say, "Loud!" in a loud voice if a sound is loud. If it's soft, he is to say, "Soft!" in a whisper. His response changes as the volume is adjusted. Start by using a radio and then vary the game by doing other things: beating a drum, knocking at the door, or using your own voice at different volume levels.

Listen and Do. Your child learns to follow a series of directions in playing this game. First start with one simple direction: "Put the key in the cup." Then give him two directions: "Put the puzzle on the table. Put the doll in the carriage." When he's able to complete two actions successfully, increase the number of directions.

Rhythm Instruments help your child appreciate differences in the quality of sounds. At the same time, banging rhythm instruments (drum, triangle, maracas) or two spoons, pots, and pans satisfies a two-year-old's need for repetition. Organizing a marching band with friends or a "concert" is also fun.

How to Use Story-time

There's far more than enjoyment to be gained from a story. Your child's vocabulary and conversation will reflect the ideas books introduce. Listening to stories increases his ability to concentrate. A story also teaches your two-year-old that events follow the specific sequence of a beginning, middle, and end. But perhaps the greatest benefit a child derives is an appreciation of books. Early pleasurable experiences with books can influence a child's attitude toward learning to read.

A two-year-old enjoys simple books that tell a story. His imagination is stirred by Little Red Riding Hood's recklessness, Goldilocks's dilemma, and the three little pigs' plight. He also relishes stories about everyday life —about daddies, mommies, little children, policemen, firemen, and animals, for example. These help him understand more about the world and his place in it.

Before you read a story to your child, become acquainted with it. Think about how you could change your voice for each character and whether there are any sound effects you could create to make it more appealing. These tactics help your child become sensitive to differences in voices and sounds and make the story more interesting.

Your child will probably request his favorites many times and quickly learn them well enough to fill in words. He'll also enjoy holding the book himself and looking at the pictures as you tell the story. Help your two-year-old expand his use of language by asking questions about the story: "What were the houses of the three pigs made of?" "Why did Goldilocks go into the bears' house?" "Who was Little Red Riding Hood going to visit?" Avoid questions that require a "yes" or "no" answer. When your child is very familiar with the story, record his telling of it on a tape recorder. Then play the tape for Grandma as a special treat to show him how proud you are of his language. Tapes of your child's language at this age become a treasured part of your family's mementos.

Usually, a story hour becomes a regular and eagerly anticipated part of your child's daily routine at this age. As your child's listening abilities develop, the stories you select can be longer and more complex. Visits to the children's room of the library can become a special occasion for your child and also extend your home bookshelf. Expose your two-year-old to different types of books. You and he might like some of the following:

ABC. New York: Grosset & Dunlap, 1975.
Jean Bethell, *Elbert Goes House Hunting.* New York: Grosset & Dunlap, 1976.
Mel Crawford, *The Cowboy Book.* New York: Golden Press, 1968.
Great Children's Stories, The Classic Volland Edition. New York: Rand McNally & Company, 1972.

Anna Jane Hayes, *See No Evil, Hear No Evil, Smell No Evil.* New York: a Sesame Street/Golden Press Book, 1975.

Syd Hoff, *When Will It Snow?* New York: Harper & Row, 1971.

Katherine Howard, *Little Bunny Follows His Nose.* New York: Golden Press, 1976.

Boche Kaplan, *Open Your Eyes.* New York: Parents' Magazine Press, 1964.

Theo LeSieg, *Come Over to My House.* New York: Random House, 1966.

John Reiss, *Colors.* Scarsdale, N.Y.: Bradbury Press, 1969.

Richard Scarry, *Please and Thank-you Book.* New York: Random House, 1973.

Richard Scarry, *Is This the House of Mistress Mouse?* New York: Golden Press, 1976.

Children's Television Workshop, *The Sesame Street 1,2,3 Storybook.* New York: Random House, 1973.

Dr. Seuss, *Dr. Seuss's ABC.* New York: Random House, 1963.

How to Use Poetry

Even though children may not understand all the words, they love to hear the melody and rhythm of poetry. As certain verses become more familiar to your child, he'll join you in saying them; soon, he may recite the entire poem. Before you know it, friends and relatives will thrill to his recital of "Humpty Dumpty," and applaud his "Jack and Jill." "Finger-plays"—poems accompanied by appropriate physical actions—are also great fun for a two-year-old. You may recall some from your childhood and enjoy teaching them to your toddler. You can also make up movements to any other poems. "The Apple Tree" lends itself to this type of activity.

> Away up high in an apple tree,
> Two red apples smiled at me.
> I shook that tree as hard as I could;
> Down came those apples,
> And mmmmm, were they good.

When you recite "Let's Make a Ball," accompany the words with hand motions.

> A little ball, a bigger ball,
> A great big ball I see;
> Now, let's count the balls we've made:
> One, two, three.

Encourage your child to follow your hand motions as you recite "Two Little Houses."

> Two little houses closed up tight;
> Open up the windows and let in the light.
> Ten little people tall and straight,
> Ready for the bus at half past eight.

Introduce your two-year-old to a wide variety of poems through collections of poetry. It's important for him to learn that books contain poems as well as stories. Also, an appreciation of poetry is a tremendous asset for a child because the richness of language and the creative way words are used in this medium help develop an extensive vocabulary. Throughout your child's school years, the way he expresses himself, both orally and in writing, will reflect the quality and quantity of words at his disposal. Start building his storehouse of words now; later he can capitalize on these verbal resources. Some collections of poetry a two-year-old might enjoy are:

> May Hill Arbuthnot and Shelton L. Root, *Time for Poetry.* Oakland, N.J.: Scott Foresman, 1968.
> *Hello Pleasant Places!* Selected by Leland B. Jacobs. New Canaan, Connecticut: Garrard Publishing Company, 1972.
> Edith Segal, *Be My Friend.* Secaucus, N.J.: The Citadel Press, 1969.
> James S. Tippett, *Crickety Cricket!* New York: Harper & Row, 1973.

How to Use Toys

Toys can provide the raw materials for self-expression. When your child devises original designs for his blocks or develops simple dialogue and actions for his dolls, he's using his imagination. Join your child in his play and become part of the world he creates with his toys. Help him develop language through your imagination-extending conversations: "Doctor, my baby is sick. Please examine her." "Could you help me, Mr. Policeman? I'm lost."

Properly selected toys can challenge, amuse, and involve your child for years, not just distract him briefly. Use your own creativity and common sense when you buy toys, and try not to be dazzled by fancy packaging or seduced by clever advertising. You're the person who knows your child best; let his interests and abilities guide your selection. Choose toys with "flexible use," which will encourage creative thinking. Toys of this sort are wonderful vehicles for your two-year-old's imagination because they can be used in a variety of ways. For example, blocks can be used to build a bridge one day and a skyscraper the next. On the other hand, toys with "rigid use" that can only be used in a limited way for a prescribed activity are a poor investment because children quickly become bored with them.

Crayons, clay, cars, trucks, dolls, farm animals, and musical instruments are toys that can interest and involve your child on many levels. Because they can be used in so many different ways, their potential for stimulating language becomes enormous: "What do you want to draw?" "How is your baby feeling today?" "Which cars are still in the garage?" "Which instruments shall we use for our song?"

When you buy toys, don't limit yourself to looking in toy stores. Hardware or office supply stores are two other excellent sources for playthings. A roll of masking tape, a ruler, a stapler, a flashlight, locks and bolts, paper clips, and chalk are examples of relatively inexpensive items that will delight your child.

How to Use a Bulletin Board

A leaf from the park or the cash register receipt from the supermarket displayed on a bulletin board helps your child remember and talk about his day: "Did we go to the supermarket or to the park before lunch?" "Whom did we meet at the supermarket?" "What did we see at the park?" Use your child's bulletin board to introduce the concept of past and future. Ticket stubs can remind him that yesterday he went to the amusement park, while the invitation tells him Janet's birthday party is coming soon. Mementos and greeting cards from holidays can also be tacked on the bulletin board and used to reminisce.

How to Use Make-Believe

An awareness of fantasy begins about this age because a two-year-old's thinking can begin to deal with the abstract. He pretends he's driving a car, fixing his tricycle, or cooking dinner. Share his world of make-believe, and you enhance his pleasure. When he offers to go shopping, tell him your list of groceries. You might suggest that he pretend to be a favorite animal. Talk about how he can crawl and say, "Meow," or "Bow-wow," or move his arms the way an elephant swings his trunk.

Start a collection of props your toddler can use in his make-believe—hats, bags, clothing, utensils, and anything else that appeals to him. When playmates visit, they'll further explore the possibilities of these "props." Encourage this creative play through your participation. Perhaps you could make a suggestion or two to get the children started: "Why don't you pretend you are mommies taking your babies for a walk?" "I think Buddy's truck has to be fixed." When they become accustomed to this kind of play and develop the necessary language, their inventiveness and originality will delight you.

How to Use Puppets

Your two-year-old begins to understand that puppets are unique toys. At first, he may only reply to the puppet with a gesture when he's directed to shake its hand, give it a kiss, or follow some instruction. Hand puppets can be used to stimulate language. The puppet can ask a question or your child can tell the puppet something. Allow him to manipulate a hand puppet if he can. If not, you move it and let your child talk to it. Accept whatever language he offers; make him feel his contribution is worthwhile. A shy child might discover that talking is easier when Bozo is there to help. At first, the dialogue will be quite simple. For example, it might go:

> Hi, I'm Bozo!
> Hi, Bozo.
> Who are you?
> I'm your new friend.
> I'm a clown.

Puppets of people or animals can talk to each other. The cow says, "Moo!" The policeman says, "Stop!" The Halloween witch says, "Trick or treat!" Improvise situations and dialogue according to your child's language ability. At this age, even one- or two-word exchanges are a fine beginning.

Making puppets is a good rainy-day project. A variety of materials can be used: paper bags, old socks, and sticks with pictures pasted on them.

How to Use Music

A simple record player and some unbreakable records are valuable additions to your child's toy shelf. You and your child will enjoy singing folk songs and nursery rhymes set to music. Songs that require a response encourage your child to use his listening skills, and the use of a drum or a spoon and pot to "accompany" the song develops a strong sense of rhythm.

These records can teach as well as amuse your child:

Alphabet and Counting Songs, Happy-Time Records, HT 1021.
Animal Alphabet, Golden Records, LP 244.

The Candy Man, Merry Records, MR 6011.
First ABC Record, Golden Records, LP 196.
45 Songs Children Love, RCA, Camden Records, CAL 1038.
Here Comes the Circus, Peter Rabbit Records, K-13.
Let's Play School, Happy-Time Records, HT 1031.
Musical Storytime, Merry Records, MR 6009.
Pete Seeger's Children's Concert at Town Hall, Harmony-Columbia Records, XSM 137195.
Susan Sings from Sesame Street, Scepter Records, SPS 584.

How to Use Television

The forceful pull of television becomes apparent at this age, so viewing should be limited to very carefully selected programs. The set shouldn't be left on for long to serve as "background noise" or as an inexpensive baby sitter. Choose programs you feel are beneficial and draw your child's attention to the show—ideally, watch it with him. When the program is over, turn the set off and involve your child in another activity.

Now is the time when viewing habits begin to develop. If your toddler always has the television set on, it'll be difficult to limit his exposure to it when he's older. Television has something to offer your child intellectually and, if properly used, can be helpful to the growth of language. Overused, it's a monster that could deprive a child of the opportunity for valuable imaginative play experiences.

The Uses of People and Places

Your two-year-old's curiosity about the world outside his home stimulates new language because the more he sees and does, the more he has to say and the more he wants to say. With a little planning and thought, a commonplace experience can become a language adventure for your child. Visits to the bank, post office, dry cleaner, and other stops on your daily round supply him with new words for his vocabulary. Explain what happens in each place. As we already noted, souvenirs, such as deposit slips, clothing tickets, and sales checks, can be collected for a bulletin board and used to stimulate conversation.

Since your child's motor control at this age is limited, he can be like the proverbial "bull in the china shop"; so don't take him where this could have disastrous consequences. He is also at the stage where he can get separated from you easily: He becomes so absorbed in his explorations that he might just roam away or not follow you. In the supermarket, he may try to discover what they're selling in the next aisle while you're waiting on the checkout line. Because of his wanderlust tendencies, your child should learn his full name and address. Rehearse the language he'll need should you—despite your best precautions—become separated, and refresh his memory from time to time.

Meeting a variety of people contributes to your child's poise as well as his language. Encourage him to speak for himself when it's appropriate: At the amusement park, he might buy his own ticket for a ride; in an elevator, he might ask for his floor; he can tell the waitress in the restaurant what flavor ice cream he craves.

Even if they're not frequent occurrences, visits to special places also help stimulate new language. Children of this age enjoy a day at the zoo, a picnic in the park, a visit to the library, a trip to the aquarium, a parade, a day at the beach, a visit to the airport, or any other place of interest you want to explore. Talking about these excursions—before, during, and after—stimulates conversation. Often, such experiences, "stored" by your child for later use, form the basis for the development of interests and hobbies.

At the beginning, most of the language stimulated by a day's outing will come from you. You describe where you're going, what you see, what you do, and whom you meet. You're your child's guide to his world and the people in it. But as you listen to the words he has to say in response to your comments, your reward will be tremendous. Take pride in the way he expresses himself and accept whatever he has to say, however he's able to say it. Instruct other members of your child's "audience" to have the same attitude.

ADVANCED ACTIVITIES

*Scrapbook

Creating and using a scrapbook increases your child's vocabulary and stimulates his imagination. Even the cutting and pasting is fun, and helps develop physical coordination. Use large colorful pictures from magazines and books. After mounting them on construction paper, shirt cardboard, or any other suitable material, collect the pictures in a looseleaf notebook.

The scrapbook encourages conversation by providing subjects to talk about. A picture of the latest-model car from a magazine advertisement could stimulate the comments: "The car is red." "It has four wheels." "I like to ride in a car." Let the scrapbooks reflect your child's interests. Some of them can be assembled according to categories in order to teach the concept that things can be arranged in groups. Foods, animals, people, or vehicles are topics a two-year-old would find interesting.

You can also add photographs of your child, family, and friends to your child's scrapbook. He enjoys talking about photographs of himself and his parents at different ages. These conversations increase his feelings of self-importance and aid in his understanding of the continuity of life. Encourage your child, if he's willing, to share his scrapbook with friends, relatives, and baby sitters; let him select his favorite pictures and tell the "story" connected with them. These are only a few of the ways to use a scrapbook, a rewarding project you and your child can work on together over a period of time.

*Colors

Your two-year-old can begin to learn the names of colors and then use these words to describe things. Matching games heighten his awareness of color. For example, show your child three different color circles: a red, blue, and yellow one. Give him another red circle and ask him to match it to one of the original three. If he's successful, do the same for the blue and yellow circles.

Another matching game involves giving your child an object of one color and asking him to find something else in the room that is the same color. The use of color words in your conversations also teaches your child this new vocabulary: "Here's your blue truck." "Bring me your brown shoes." When you build with different color blocks, mention the names of the colors: "I need a blue block for the roof." "Let's put a red block on top of the tower."

*Numbers

Your use of number words—primarily, "one," "two," "three," and "many"—helps your child understand quantities: "You have two eyes." "Bring me three crayons." "I see many cars on the street." "Do you want one or two cookies?" Your child's use of these words in spoken language will be limited, but he should now learn to understand them on a receptive level.

How Many? Place groups of objects on a table in different-number groups: three spoons, two forks, one cup, four straws, for instance. Then ask your child, "How many forks are on the table?" He must gather the objects and count them, though with your help at first.

Give Me the _____ can be played with the same objects as in the previous activity. Ask your child to give you specific numbers of the same object, but not necessarily the entire group: "Give me two spoons." "Give me three straws."

7.

The Power of Language: Three to Four Years

"Brett wants to do everything for himself, now."

"Connie likes to pretend she's the mommy and I'm the child."

"Sandy insists on wearing that same red sweater every day."

"Johnny gets very insulted when I refer to him as 'the baby.'"

Comments like the ones above are common in the homes of three-year-olds. Brace yourself for another year of big changes! This year your child assumes more and more responsibility, and takes over some tasks you once feared would be yours forever. Now he helps himself to fruit from the refrigerator, chooses his own clothes each morning (so what if the striped jeans clash with that plaid T-shirt?), and is determined to make up his very own guest list for the upcoming birthday bash.

Your three-year-old *knows* there's a world of difference between the way he used to be and the way he is now. "I'm not a baby anymore!" he asserts. And he's proud of the things he can do now and of the fascinating lessons of life he's already mastered.

But at other times he may decide he's not quite ready to relinquish the prerogatives of babyhood. He alternates between baby behavior and being a big boy (or girl), sensing the advantages of sustaining both states. He'll need time, sympathy, and support to make progress and resolve these conflicting patterns. Inevitably, as the benefits of being big grow apparent, more mature behavior will become the general rule.

Still, the transition can be a rocky one. Some days, Lenny goes confidently off to join his play group. Other days he clings to his mother or insists on taking along his security blanket for morale. Lenny's mother wisely accepts both types of behavior, but she also makes clear which path he ought to choose by complimenting him whenever his actions bear the earmarks of maturity.

With proper stimulation, your three-year-old can learn an incredible number of things on his own (although, of course, at each age there's a natural readiness for certain types of learning). Nancy didn't wait for her parents to teach her the letters of the alphabet. She learned them —with electronic assistance, to be sure, but on her own initiative—while watching a morning TV program.

Your three-year-old has a broad awareness of the world beyond his home. You'll probably be surprised, even shocked, to learn how much he already knows. One fall day, Marcy and her mother were at the zoo. When they reached the bears' den, Marcy asked where those grizzlies planned to sleep through the winter months. Her mother was flabbergasted to learn how much Marcy knew about animal hibernation; it seemed her baby sitter had read her a story about a bear with a penchant for cold-weather comfort. Marcy's mother realized then and there that she no longer knew the full range of her daughter's knowledge.

As your child gathers information from a growing number of sources, he may begin to quote newly acquired authorities. Gina's big brother informed her that butterflies develop from caterpillars; her friend Sally assured her that ice cream never really melts; her nursery school teacher taught her an easy trick for slipping into her clumsy lumber jacket. And television, of course, for all its bad press, can provide an alert child with much information.

Language—A Flexible Tool

During this year the importance of language to your child goes far beyond the mere naming of things and the expression of needs: He uses it now to voice his opinions, issue directions, weave tales, fantasize, recount the day's events, share thoughts and feelings, brag, argue, reason, bully, persuade, and plead. He decides what he wants to wear, with whom he wishes to play, which story he wants you to read. He learns to describe his feelings with some precision—openly expressing joy when you surprise him with a gift, and overtly expressing his anger when you snatch the box of matches away from him. Now he can tell you just where it hurts, instead of displaying general crankiness.

Memories become an integral part of your three-year-old's language. He finds excitement in recalling things past and takes pride in chattering about old happenings. Out of a clear blue sky, he may remind you of that fun-filled week at the beach, or the painful moment at the zoo when his balloon sailed off into the sky. Sometimes his recollections may give you a jolt. Annie and her father drove downtown for a shopping spree. When her father found a spot to park, Annie instructed him with great firmness to feed a coin into the parking meter without delay. She reminded him of a time last summer when he'd neglected to do so—and of the traffic ticket he found on his car later that afternoon. Annie's father was amazed at her ability to remember something that happened so long ago.

Not infrequently, you may find your child's memory more accurate than your own. When Jenny and her father bought a pair of goldfish, the pet-store salesman gave them explicit instructions about the fish's care and feeding. Next afternoon, as Jenny's father was preparing a second meal for the fish, Jenny reminded him that they were only to be fed once a day. A telephone call to the pet shop confirmed that Jenny's recall of the feeding rule was accurate.

Don't ever forget how important a role language plays in developing relationships with people. Your three-year-old is so curious about other children—he wants to know not only their names and where they live but what their place is in his life. Spending time with playmates is most important at this stage in your child's development. Even if his date book begins to crowd out your own calendar, remember that this social life nourishes him with imaginative play and an increased sharing of experiences, both factual and fantasized. Your child's language reflects this kind of enrichment. Through contacts with friends, he acquires new words and new phrases.

When alone, he uses language to enhance his play. He chats with his toys, confides in his pets, and may strike up a one-way conversation with television characters. You may overhear him giving directions and organizing activities aloud. Abby, a three-year-old, is convinced that her cat hangs on to her every word. Talking to animals, or even to inanimate objects, is one way your child practices relating to others. It's a healthy exercise of imagination—and stretches use of language.

If you're attentive, you may notice that your child imitates some of your own phrases and inflections. That shouldn't come as a surprise, since you're his primary language teacher. Learning any new skill requires mastering certain basics. When you take a course in cooking, you're likely to follow closely your instructor's motions in chopping, seasoning, basting, and baking. Language learning isn't very different. It involves mastering fundamental skills, which your child learns from *you*.

When Words Come in Floods

Three-year-olds are a garrulous bunch! They're fascinated by the sounds of their own voices and sometimes they tend to ramble on as interminably as a filibustering senator's monologue! An idea that might be fully expressed in a single sentence is expanded, embroidered, embellished. Nicky, who is five, invited his friend to play. "Can you come to my house after school?" he asked. But his three-year-old sibling found it necessary to add, "Yes come to our house . . . come to play . . . please come . . . I have a new tow truck . . . come to see my truck . . . I'll let you play with my truck if you come . . . it dumps sand. . . ."

When your child is going through this talkative stage, do spend a great deal of time listening—with patience. As a member of his captive audience, your role is to participate. Allow yourself to act as a sounding board. Comment on what he has to say. Add your own thoughts. Bear in mind that, during this stage, it's difficult for your three-year-old to economize on words. Be forbearing and understanding.

Now Language Takes Shape

Your three-year-old's language has a grown-up ring to it, even though neither his pronunciation nor his grammar is anything like letter-perfect. His vocabulary, meanwhile, increases apace, reflecting home influences and outside experiences. Claire's parents were pleased to hear her rattle off words such as "kiln," "ceramics," and "potter's wheel." The source of this specialized vocabulary was her friend Maria's mother, an amateur potter. Whenever Claire visited Maria's house, Maria's mother encouraged the girls to inspect her studio and handle the wet clay.

By now, nouns, verbs, pronouns, adjectives, and adverbs are all part of your child's language. With this richer language, he's able to express thoughts and observations with some precision. What a thrill when you first hear, "Mommy, you look beautiful!" or "Daddy, you must be the strongest man in all the world!" Your child's language becomes more exact as he learns to pinpoint the right word for each occasion. Show him how to characterize the elephant as "enormous" or even "gigantic" instead of merely "big"; help him describe an ant as "tiny" or "small" instead of just "little." In this way his vocabulary stretches, and with it grows his ability to express his thoughts more precisely and more vividly.

Infantile language patterns start to disappear. He begins to use pronouns more appropriately as he follows your model. "Me want ice cream" is replaced by "I want ice cream." "Him gave the toy to me" becomes "He gave the toy to me." Of course, your child still may require more time to hone his articulation of certain difficult speech sounds. The *tr* in "trick" is tricky, the *th* in "something" still may defeat a three-year-old, and the *st* in "most" takes some doing to master. Certain words remain troublesome because of the way individual sounds are combined to form them. In some words, individual sounds may be pronounced correctly, while in others the same sounds may cause problems. "Breakfast" may continue to emerge as "breaksist," "pisgetti" may long remain a substitute for "spaghetti," and "sukermarket" may serve as the best available replica of "supermarket."

In addition, your three-year-old's sentence structure has grown more complex. No longer does he merely protest, "I don't want to go to bed." Now he introduces reason to go with his newly acquired coherence. "I don't want to go to bed," he may argue, "because I took my nap today. So, I'm not tired." You'd better sharpen your debating skills at this point. They may come in handy as you find yourself matching wits with a worthy adversary.

Your child's language now reflects his understanding of the past, present, and future. His use of tense indicates he is sorting out the time lines of his life and attempting to place experiences in their proper sequence. Expressing himself in the past tense may still present some obstacles. As we noted before, a child tends to add "ed" indiscriminately to the end of a verb to indicate something that's already happened. He may persist in saying "finded" instead of "found," "eated" for "ate," or "runned" in place of "ran." Unfortunately, there's more to English grammar than the mere dictates of logic!

You're Ever the Model

At every age, an important part of language learning entails having an appropriate model. If you address your child now in a more complex, more adult fashion, his own speech will gradually become less babyish. Encourage this trend whenever you engage in conversation—but do make allowances for his inevitable lapses.

Your attitude toward your three-year-old's language should continue to be accepting and supportive. In his earlier years, when his attempts were less successful, your understanding gave your child the confidence to develop language skills. Now, although his language appears more grown-up, certain sounds may still be difficult to master. It's quite important to allow your child to pursue language learning at his own pace.

One stifling day in summer, Norman tore into his house shouting, "Mommy, the fire hydent is skirting water." His mother led him back into the street to inspect the geyser. She wisely decided not to put a damper on her son's excitement by correcting his speech. Instead, she took the opportunity to repeat his own words correctly. "The fire hydrant is squirting cool and wonderful water," she told him. "Let's get your bathing suit and go splashing."

My, What Attentive Ears You Have!

Your child is becoming a sophisticated listener. He listens now with more comprehension and is capable of finer sound discrimination. Nuances of language, plays on words, even the most outrageous puns are likely to amuse him no end. Words with the same sound but different meanings fascinate a three-year-old. "The wind blew my blue hat away," may produce paroxysms of laughter.

As your child's listening ability develops, he learns to be more selective. If he doesn't care for what you say, he may "tune you out" now, pretending not to hear you.

This may not be rudeness; your child may be acting defensively, helping himself to deal more effectively with a disagreeable situation or allowing himself more time to plan his own reaction. Adults use the same sort of device when they automatically ask, "What did you say?" to give themselves extra time before answering.

When your child turns a deaf ear, simply repeat what you said. It may prove more to his liking the second time. If this type of tuning-out behavior grows into a full-sized problem, wait until you're sure you have his complete attention before asking a question or giving a direction. When your child realizes you *know* he hears you loud and clear, he's less likely to use this ploy.

By dint of sharpened listening skills, your child becomes a more creative and a more critical audience. He should become a more appreciative listener as well. At this stage, he may develop a stubborn fondness for a certain song or phonograph record, which he insists on hearing again and again. He may learn the song by heart and even begin to prefer his own unique version of it.

Encourage your child to verbalize his penchant for certain kinds of music, to tell you why a particular song has so much appeal. Try to expose him to other kinds of recorded sounds, especially if he really seems to be stuck in a one-kind-of-music groove. It's not too early to introduce him to bel canto and classical gems, to wean him away subtly from bongo-drum or rock-and-roll infatuation. After all, he's at an age when his musical tastes are beginning to develop and to jell.

As the world of your three-year-old grows in complexity, his ability to listen becomes crucial; it's a vital tool in coping with new places, new experiences, and newly introduced people. He can only benefit from the knowledge and insights of others, provided he listens thoroughly and develops an open mind. The child who learns to integrate verbal information correctly and efficiently is well equipped to handle life's challenges.

The Vital Link: Language and Thought

Now that your three-year-old has mastered most of the fundamentals of language, he can focus more directly on its content. With the maturing of his thought processes, a profound change occurs in his ability to grasp abstract ideas.

Randy was intrigued by the gradations between hot and warm temperatures. The extremes of hot and cold were by now familiar concepts, but the notion that there could be an in-between was fascinating. He kept pressing his mother to cite examples of warm objects; he wanted to know how some things change from hot to warm, warm to cold, and back again. His mother's patient explanations helped Randy realize that words refer to concepts as well as concrete things.

Frankness—indeed, bluntness—is characteristic of your three-year-old's thinking. He rarely censors the content of his language; he may blurt out your most intimate secrets or embarrassing queries. If it's something that's on his mind, it's already on the tip of his tongue.

Your child's language offers unmistakable clues to the workings of his mind. When Kelly's mother told her to play harmoniously with her friend Jay, Kelly rebelled, informing her mother, "Jay is not my friend. He wasn't at my birthday party." Kelly's mother explained that Jay had not been at the party because he hadn't yet moved into the neighborhood. Kelly was led to understand there was no logical reason why Jay couldn't become her playmate even though he hadn't yet entered her circle of friends at the time of her last birthday.

Your child can now discuss events in the abstract without being bound by the here-and-now. Use this ability to prepare him for the unfamiliar and unexpected. With your help, he can develop the necessary vocabulary to cope with new experiences.

Hillary was about to take her first airplane trip. The prospect of flying set her all atingle, but she didn't know what precisely to expect. Her mother conditioned her for the projected trip by acting out some of the experiences that were in store. "Fasten your seat belts," she told Hillary, in a dry-run exercise at home, "we're ready for takeoff." Hillary buckled one of her mother's belts around her waist. "The pilot is starting his engine now," her mother went on. "We're beginning to move along the runway. The plane is slowly lifting off the ground. See how small the houses and cars below seem. Now we can no longer see the ground. We're going higher and higher into the clouds, above the clouds." At lunchtime, Hillary's mother pretended to be a stewardess, serving lunch on a tray. On another occasion, she lined up chairs to form an aisle. Hillary learned she would have to stay in her seat during most of her trip, except for visits to the bathroom. Running was frowned upon—and, please, no dancing in the aisles under any pretext!

One night, Hillary's father assumed the role of pilot and issued a progress report to his passengers. He gave Hillary some pointers on cockpit operations. By the time Hillary boarded her first plane, she had just about earned her wings. Because of her familiarity with in-flight procedures, she had developed a sense of security and serenity. She also had acquired the language and information necessary to appreciate the new experience fully.

Your three-year-old becomes enchanted with the world of make-believe. (Imagination can be such a valuable asset in language growth as well as in life in general!) Once Alan's father has left the house on a weekday morning, Alan calls out to his mother, "Goodbye, dear, I'm off to the office now." Alan's mother dutifully replies, "Have a good day, then. And what would you like for dinner?" The pretense continues as Alan lists his menu choices. Alan knows it's all a delightful sham, but it pleases him, and, more important, he's learning new ways to use language.

Questions—and Some Querulousness

As the scope of your three-year-old's curiosity widens, his questions increase. He has an enormous appetite for acquiring new knowledge. Asking is his way of garnering information and finding out how to cope with new situations. Try to help your child find his own answers. When he asks, "Do I have to wear a hat today?" you might suggest, "Let's find out how cold it is outside." Allow him to express his own opinion on the subject, then together test how cold the windowpane feels, consult the thermometer, or put your hands outside the window. If your mutual opinion is that it's cold, he wears his hat; if not, the hat can stay behind in the closet. Don't directly answer your child's question when there's a possibility of his finding his own response.

Sometimes your child's questions may relate to experiences you didn't share. Pamela's nursery school class made a field trip to the local fire station, where she was mesmerized by the fire engines and the glistening brass poles. She came home with dozens of questions for her parents about fire engine procedures and fire control. These queries were Pamela's way of sharing the trip with her mother and father.

Your child may begin to concentrate questions on one particular area once his interests become more developed. Evan was totally absorbed by anything related to construction. Whenever he passed the site of some new building, he insisted on stopping to watch the progress of the cranes, derricks, and bricklayers. He wanted to know the names of the pieces of machinery, the way cement was mixed, how bricks were made, and countless other technical details. His parents, though they began to feel like engineering consultants, encouraged Evan's avid interest by allowing him to talk with construction workers and finding children's books about building.

At times your child will pose a question to which he already knows the answer. Such questions shouldn't be ignored; they may conceal a significant message. Perhaps your child is feeling lonely or "left out of the picture." His questions may be his way of pleading, "Talk to me. Pay attention to me." Your three-year-old may need your companionship as well as the information you can impart.

While Jonathan ate his breakfast, his mother generally used the time to straighten the house. Jonathan never was able to sit still at the table during this time. He was constantly popping up to pose a question: "Where did you put the cereal? . . . What are we going to do today? . . . Can I have a straw with my milk?" Before long, Jonathan's mother began to realize that the answers he sought were far less important than assuring him of her company at breakfast. She learned to postpone her household chores, to sit at the table with her son while sipping a second cup of coffee.

When your child's questions begin to focus on abstract topics, you may expect some whopping challenges. "Why is the sky blue?" is a typical brain teaser that occurs to many children. Also: "Why do I get hungry?"

"How do I wake up?" "Do animals talk to each other?" —and ad infinitum. These are questions worthy of the most serious scholar. You may find yourself honing your own brainpower, and maybe doing some research on the sly, to cope with this battery of complex questions.

"What if?" is a phrase that now becomes a staple of your child's vocabulary. He's concerned with the order and the stability of life. Faced with puzzling emotional situations, his fears and confusions surface in these "What if?" sticklers, reflecting his urgent need for reassurance.

When Carrie's dog, Lollypop, was obliged to spend several days in the animal hospital, Carrie's questions centered on her pet's separation from the family fold. "What if she gets hungry?" she wanted to know. "What if she misses me?" "What if she is lonely?" The concerns behind these questions were obvious, but Carrie also asked questions of subtler significance. She was hesitant now about parting from her mother to attend nursery school. She wondered who would take care of *her* if she was hurt, who would feed *her* if she was hungry.

Carrie's mother was, at first, puzzled by this turn in her daughter's questions. After some thought, however, she was able to relate Carrie's concerns to Lollypop's ordeal away from home. She then offered Carrie all the reassurance and support she needed. If you look beyond the immediate context in which some of your child's questions are asked, you may be able to glean some valuable insights about his emotional state.

Your three-year-old is very curious about his own body and how it functions. He's already aware of the differences between the sexes, and between the bodies of children and adults. Answers to his candid questions should be at his own level and as forthright as possible. It isn't necessary to meander beyond the immediate scope of his questions. Be sure you understand what information he is really seeking. Remember that old story about the little boy who wanted to know where he came from? His parents obligingly provided him with an explicit explanation of the reproductive organs, fertilization, gestation, and birth. Once they'd exhausted their storehouse of information on these subjects, their little boy exclaimed, "I only wanted to know if I came from Philadelphia or Pittsburgh!"

You ought to decide in advance what you plan to say when it's time for an exposition on the birds and the bees. Some parents are more comfortable with clinical language, but whatever vocabulary you choose, honesty is the most important ingredient of your "little lecture." Children are very perceptive about their parents' feelings; when parents are at ease in their discussions of sex, that attitude immediately communicates itself.

Language As a Tool in Reasoning

The baby who realizes that bellowing will bring his mother flying with a warm bottle, the toddler who goes on asking "What's that? What's that?" without any mercy, and the three-year-old who cons his buddy into playing the game of his choice, all have something in common. Each has learned the power of language (or simple sustained sounds) to bring rewards—nourishment, in one instance; knowledge, in another; and the satisfaction of "having things my way," in the third.

Reason develops—and is refined—through the use of language, and as your youngster learns to articulate his feelings of happiness, joy, sorrow, anger, or disappointment, he can discuss these states of mind with adults. The vocabulary adults use in replying may still float over his head, but new words and concepts soon become familiar; one day he himself will put them to use.

When Mary came home from the playground, she realized she'd thoughtlessly abandoned her favorite doll on a park bench; she became quite upset. Mary and her mother returned at once to search for the doll, but in vain. By now Mary was heartbroken; she broke down in tears. Putting an arm around her sobbing daughter, Mary's mother talked about some of the feelings she knew Mary must be experiencing:

"I know how disappointed you are we couldn't find Sadie," she said. "It's quite a sad thing to lose your very closest doll. You'll miss her very much. I become unhappy too whenever I lose something dear to me—and then I wish I had been more careful." The mother's empathy and understanding (and even the gentle chiding) helped the child sort out her own feelings. Mary began to comprehend her emotions while learning the words to properly describe them.

Parents can do a lot to convince children of the advantages of reacting with reason, not just with raw emotion. Even at an early age, reasoning and logic can become factors in a parent-child relationship. Intelligent discussions, reasoned compromise, and the offering of acceptable options can go a long way toward avoiding family flare-ups and a bad case of the generation gap.

One morning, when Justin and his father went shopping in the local toy store, Justin fell headlong in love with a model airplane. It certainly was a handsome specimen, but it was delicately constructed and therefore Justin's father vetoed its purchase. Justin burst into tears of self-pity. His father thereupon carefully explained that he had no ·objection to buying his son an airplane, but that the one he admired was much too fragile to survive very long. It wasn't sturdy enough to fly and would surely splinter with its first crash to earth. After the father had spelled out the advantages of investing in a more durable model, Justin also began to see the wisdom of that alternative. Justin's father was not only instructing his son in the uses of language, he was providing a lesson in resolving a conflict maturely at the same time.

As your three-year-old gains in self-confidence, he may want to do (or have) inappropriate things for his age. Again, language can effectively curtail unreasonable demands or postpone overreaching desires. Sherry decided she wanted to walk to nursery school unaccompanied after she noticed the older children on her block making their way each morning without benefit of parents. Instead of flatly denying her request, Sherry's mother talked with her about the realities of going it alone. There was the danger of crossing heavily trafficked streets, and the problems of remembering the right route and even being able to reach the school building's doorknob and push open the heavy metal door. Sherry began to have second thoughts about her impetuous plans; she agreed to wait until she was enrolled in elementary school before abandoning the morning walks with her mother.

Using Language to Cope with Problems

Problem solving is an important skill at every age: The toddler who learns that mounting a stool will put him in reach of the cookie jar may glow with no less pride than the computer-aided astronomer who succeeds in calculating the walking distance to Mars. Use language to teach your child how to recognize and describe his daily problems, and how to choose among alternative solutions in resolving them. Don't fret about "overtalking" a situation; repetition helps children, as well as adults, to clarify their thoughts.

Karen felt the urge to try out her friend Ellen's tricycle and became very upset when Ellen obstinately refused her that privilege. After days of frustration, Karen sulked about having to visit the playground where Ellen held court. Karen's mother discussed the problem with her daughter. Together they explored three options. Karen could stop going to the playground, Karen's mother could prevail on Ellen's mother to accommodate Karen, or Karen could return to the playground with a toy she might lend Ellen in exchange for a ride on her tricycle.

Karen and her mother agreed that the last choice was the most realistic. Next afternoon, Karen returned to the playground with her favorite scooter. In exchange for letting Ellen try the scooter, Karen got to chug away on Ellen's tricycle. A craggy problem had been resolved, thanks to mother and daughter considering the various solutions in an atmosphere of calm and reason.

The ability to use language effectively is a very important skill, a vital tool in the increasingly complex world of the three-year-old whose expanding social contacts contribute to a new sense of self-awareness. As his attention span increases, your child begins to enjoy a wide range of challenging activities. He becomes ever more curious, ever more involved. His desire to participate in new experiences grows by leaps and bounds. Parents must not neglect their increasing opportunities to motivate, challenge, and stimulate their children.

ACTIVITIES

How to Use Rhyming

The following activities increase your child's awareness of the sounds in words. He learns new language as you help him understand which rhyming words are real and which are nonsense words. These activities also introduce him to the concept of word families, which is so important in learning to read.

Rhyming Words helps your child identify words that sound alike. Give him three words, two of which rhyme. Ask him to tell you the one that doesn't belong. Vary the position of the nonrhyming word: cap, lap, hill/ make, top, take/ sad, bed, red. When your child is able to guess the correct word, increase the number of words to four: stop, hop, mop, show/ match, car, catch, patch/ fork, neat, treat, seat.

Rhyming Riddles requires your child to answer a question with a rhyme: "I'm thinking of something that rhymes with tall, call, and fall. It's round and it bounces. What is it?" The word your child must guess, of course, is "ball." Other examples: "I'm thinking of something that rhymes with well, tell, and fell. You ring it and it makes a sound. What is it?" "I'm thinking of something that rhymes with hat, sat, and fat. It's an animal and says 'meow.' What is it?"

Rhyming Poems develops the ability to complete a couplet with a rhyming word. Give your child a two-line descriptive jingle, but omit the last word in the second line and ask your child to fill it in:

> I never stand still
> When I run down a _____ (hill).

I take my glass to the sink
To get a cold _____ (drink).

I jump from my seat
And stand on my _____ (feet).

I cross the floor
To open the _____ (door).

Rhyming Lists helps your child learn to make up his own rhymes. Give your child a word and ask him to tell you all the words he can think of that rhyme with it. Choose words for which there are many different possible rhymes, such as hat, bell, man, and ball. As your child's skill increases, choose words that are more difficult to rhyme.

Listening Exercises

The listening activities that follow are designed to expand your three-year-old's auditory memory and help him recognize and evaluate different dimensions of sound quality. They also require a more challenging use of language.

Sound Patterns is a game that teaches your child to remember and imitate what he hears. Clap your hands twice and ask your child to do the same. Vary the rhythm and number of claps: fast, fast/ fast, fast, slow/ slow, fast, fast/ slow, slow, fast, fast/ and so on. Sometimes, your child can clap out the rhythm for you to copy. Rhythm instruments can also be used for this activity.

Near and Far develops judgment about the distance of sounds. Have your child sit in a chair with his back to you. First make a sound near him and then one from across the room. Tell your child to say "near" if the sound is right behind him and "far" if the sound is further away. Use a variety of sound-making objects for this game: whistle, bell, rhythm instruments, drum, or gong.

Animal Sounds teaches your child to listen for key words. As you tell a simple story about one animal, ask your child to make the appropriate sound every time you mention the word for the animal. In the following story, for example, your child says "bow-wow" whenever you say the word "dog."

"Rusty is a brown-and-white dog [child says 'bow-wow']. Rusty lives with a girl named Margo. The little dog ['bow-wow'] has his own house in the back yard. Whenever Margo calls her dog ['bow-wow'], Rusty comes running out of the house. Margo loves her dog ['bow-wow'] very much. Dogs ['bow-wow'] are such wonderful pets."

Make up your own stories about familiar animals, varying the part of the sentence in which the key word appears. When your child is ready for it, increase the number of animals that appear in your story:

"Farmer Gray had a cow ['moo'] named Becky, and a pig ['oink-oink'] named Harold. Becky and Harold were as friendly as a cow ['moo'] and a pig ['oink-oink'] could possibly be. Every morning, Becky, the cow ['moo'], looked for Harold, the pig ['oink-oink']. Usually, she found the pig ['oink-oink'] eating breakfast in the corner of the barnyard. After Farmer Gray milked his cow ['moo'], Becky joined her friend Harold. The cow ['moo'] and the pig ['oink-oink'] had breakfast together: corn husks for the pig ['oink-oink'] and hay for the cow ['moo']."

Copycats helps your child remember what he hears. Teach him a simple song or poem such as "Row, Row, Row Your Boat" by saying a line or phrase from it and having him repeat the segment after you. After your child repeats such segments several times, he probably will have memorized them. Try more difficult material such as "Yankee Doodle" when you feel he can memorize it.

Story Fill-in teaches your child to follow a story and participate in the narration. Read a story containing a phrase or word that is often repeated. Your child fills in the phrase or word at the appropriate point in the story. He must listen closely for his cue. "The Three Little Pigs," "Three Billy Goats Gruff," "The Gingerbread Man," and "Chicken Little" are particularly good stories for this activity.

Sounds Around Us develops the ability to perceive and respond to subtle sounds in our environment. Ask your child to close his eyes and tell you what he hears. At first, he may simply say, "Nothing," but ask him to try again. You might mention one sound you hear in order to get him started: "I hear a car in the street." Try this game in different rooms of the house, while driving, at the playground, in the supermarket, and walking in the street. The more he plays this game, the better your child becomes at it and the more he'll enjoy it. He'll suggest other places to try his listening skill.

How to Use a Scrapbook

Scrapbooks can be used to refine a three-year-old's understanding of categories. Selecting the material for a scrapbook heightens his awareness of the subtleties of language. Ask for your child's suggestions as to what kind of scrapbook to start. If he's involved with cars, for instance, find pictures of different kinds of cars.

Animal Scrapbook

A scrapbook about animals might include pictures of those not usually found in zoos. Try to find unusual examples from the animal world. Your three-year-old delights in learning to pronounce the words emu, aardvark, koala, and orangutan. As his interests expand, the types of scrapbooks he wants to make change.

Concepts Scrapbook

Scrapbooks can be compiled around concepts such as things of the same size or color. A scrapbook about big things could include pictures of skyscrapers, ocean liners, mountains, and whales. Another about cold things would feature icicles, refrigerators, snow, and an air conditioner. A project on the color red might show an apple, lipstick, a red dress, and a red car.

Opposites Scrapbook

Opposites can also be shown in a scrapbook. First explain the idea of the mutually exclusive qualities of opposites: If it's hot, it can't be cold; if it's high, it can't be low. Then help your child compile the scrapbook. A picture of a baby and one of a grandmother illustrates young and old. Decide what pair of opposites a picture or pictures illustrates: The chandelier on the ceiling and the rug on the floor demonstrate up and down. A steaming cup of coffee and a dish of ice cream depict hot and cold. If your child isn't sure what category a particular picture belongs under, talking about it can be helpful. As you discuss the reasons for his choices, you're helping your child acquire the language he needs to express his ideas. He also learns that talking about an idea often helps clarify it.

How to Build a Body Image

Your three-year-old's awareness of himself is sharpened as he forms a mental picture of how he looks and what his body can do. The names and functions of the parts of his body as well as how they work together become part of his self-image. He begins to understand how his body is related to other people and objects: His arms can hug a friend. His foot can kick a ball.

People Puzzles help your child understand the placement of the different parts of his body. Draw a large circle. Give your child cutouts of the parts of the face (eyes, nose, mouth, ears, teeth) and ask him to put them in the correct place on the circle.

Then draw an outline of the human figure. Ask your child to put cutouts of the parts of the body on the picture. Your cutouts can be of hands, feet, parts of the face, hair, knee, shoulder, and anything else your child might be familiar with.

Can You Do This? reinforces your child's idea of how his body functions in space. After he's able to follow directions for large body movements, ask him to try smaller ones: "Open your mouth. Blink your eyes. Bend your knee. Wiggle your thumb. Shrug your shoulders." Perhaps he can suggest other actions. When he can do these as well, alternate large and small body movements: "Jump up and down. Clap your hands. Run across the room. Turn your head."

Jigsaw Puzzles made from life-size drawings can help your child understand the relationship of the parts of his body to one another. Trace the outline of his body on a large sheet of paper and draw in the features. The various parts of the figure can be as detailed as your child chooses to make them; everything from eyelashes to toenails can be included. Next, cut out the outline, and then cut the figure into irregular pieces to form a jigsaw puzzle. As you fit it together, experiment with putting different parts of the body in different places: "How would you walk if your foot was on your stomach? Why don't we have a hand on our face? How would you use your mouth if it was on your knees?" These questions stimulate your child's imagination as well as his language. He'll want to ask you other "silly questions" about his body.

If anything is troubling your child about himself, it may come out during this kind of discussion. Perhaps he wishes he was stronger, not so short, could run faster, or had curly hair. By talking about these feelings, you can explain that everyone is a unique individual, quite different from anyone else in the whole world. We all have things about ourselves that make us very proud and other features we would like to change.

Using Role Play

Role play provides a positive outlet for fantasy and creativity. Children like to pretend they're someone or something else. They make believe they're Mommy or Daddy, a cat or a dog, or a favorite character from television. Daddy's old coat and briefcase, Mommy's straw hat and handbag, or other suitable objects enhance role play.

Your child's first experience with role play probably will involve a commonplace activity he has observed. He may ring up his sales on an imaginary cash register or pretend to hammer a nail. You might also hear him mimicking your expressions, perhaps saying, "Fill it up, please," as he passes on his tricycle. Capitalize on this natural instinct by joining in the role play. After you "fill his gas tank," you might tell him the price of the gas, wipe his "windshield," or ask if he wants you to "check under the hood." In this way, his tentative explorations are enriched.

Role play allows your child to express his impressions and thoughts. Role play is one way he can build a concept of reality. Don't be surprised when you hear him speak to his pet or doll the way you speak to him. Role play encourages your child to test his viewpoint as well as his language and gives him the opportunity to see the world from another's point of view. Through your interaction, you can also modify his behavior, if necessary.

How to Use Children's Theater

Take advantage of any opportunities to have your child experience the magic of children's theater. Your three-year-old will enjoy plays dramatizing new tales as well as stories he has heard many times. Vocabulary grows as theater language—"program," "intermission," "audience," "script"—is discussed. During the play, your child must pay close attention and listen carefully to the actors. Learning to be a responsive member of an audience increases his attention span.

After the show, your three-year-old may want to talk about the play. Show an interest in what he has to say by asking questions and making specific comments: "The witch sounds scary." "How was the princess rescued?" "What did the prince do to the witch?" When you listen attentively, your child feels as though he has something worthwhile to contribute.

Using Puppets

Puppets are valuable in encouraging language growth because a puppet suggests, "Talk for me." Possibly from our experience with viewing puppets, when we pick one up, our first reaction is to have it say something.

The child who is shy may have no difficulty when the puppet is doing the talking. Puppets also promote an awareness of voice quality: Often when speaking through a puppet, we tend to change the pitch and volume of our voices.

Puppets can sometimes be used as an extension of role play to handle a sensitive problem. A child who is having difficulty controlling his aggressive behavior may be receptive to a debate between puppets about the comparative merits of grabbing a toy versus asking to have a turn with it.

Using Storybooks

As your child's attention span increases, choose longer, more challenging books. But be sure to stop reading while he's still entranced! If the story is too long, spread the reading out over several days. Build suspense by stopping at exciting parts.

There may be certain subjects your child prefers hearing about. Allow him to select books on these favorite topics. At the same time, encourage him to expand his reading list so he can learn that books are a wonderful source of information as well as being enjoyable.

The books you select can reflect your viewpoint about social issues. For instance, some children's books are more traditional than others with regard to women's roles. If you want your child to understand and appreciate the many options open to women today, choose books showing women successfully pursuing careers. There are also books you can share with your child that deal with children from minority groups. The message of books with children of different races and backgrounds in the story and illustrations is one of brotherhood: children of different races playing and learning together.

Your child should be taught to care for and respect books. One way to enhance their value in his eyes is to give books as presents. The following list is an indication of how many books written for three-year-olds inform while they entertain.

Anne Alexander, *ABC of Cars and Trucks.* New York: Doubleday, 1956.

Norman Bridwell, *Clifford Takes a Trip.* New York: Scholastic Books, 1966.

Gwendolyn Brooks, *The Tiger Who Wore White Gloves.* Chicago: Third World Press, 1974.

Joy Troth Friedman, *Look Around and Listen.* New York: Grosset & Dunlap, 1974.

Rosemary Garland, *My Bedtime Book of Two-Minute Stories.* New York: Grosset & Dunlap, 1976.

Annie Ingle, *Big City Book.* New York: Platt & Munk Publishers, 1975.

Joe Kaufman, *Joe Kaufman's Book About Busy People.* New York: Golden Press, 1975.

Joe Lasker, *Mother Can Do Anything.* Chicago: Albert Whitman & Company, 1974.

Robert Pierce, *What If?* New York: Golden Press, 1969.

Seymour Reit, *The Easy How-to Book.* New York: Golden Press, 1975.

Joyce Richards, *How Come . . .? Easy Answers to Hard Questions.* New York: Platt & Munk Publishers, 1975.

Kent Salisbury, *Tell a Tall Tale*. New York: Golden Press, 1966.

Richard Scarry, *Great Big Schoolhouse*. New York: Random House, 1969.

Dr. Seuss, *Green Eggs and Ham*. New York: Random House, 1960.

John Steptoe, *Birthday*. New York: Holt, Rinehart & Winston, Inc., 1972.

How to Use Storytelling

Sometimes, tell your child an original story instead of reading one. After you've read enough children's books, you can probably combine elements from different stories. If not, read a book, familiarize yourself with the story, and tell it in your own words.

Another source of new tales is your own childhood. Your child will be thrilled to hear about when Mommy and Daddy were little. He wants to know what Grandma and Grandpa were like as parents and all of your childhood memories.

You and your child may also create stories about a fantasy character or group of people with clearly defined physical qualities and life-styles. The stories may border on the absurd, but somehow they eventually touch base with reality. As you keep adding new "chapters," they become an ongoing saga. Often these stories reflect the unique circumstances of the family, and that is why adults cherish memories of them as a special part of childhood.

Your child might be able to make up stories of his own. Even though they may be short and somewhat disjointed, enjoy them as a delightful part of communication with him. Sometimes, you and your child tell a story together. You can start and when you stop, he continues the action. Then, when his imagination falters, you take over the narration for a little while. Stop at a turning point in the story, and have him tell you what he thinks happens next. Alternate in this way until a satisfactory ending is reached. Don't plan the story too far ahead in your mind. Let your imagination roam free.

Using Poetry

Reading poems to your child helps him develop a sensitivity toward language. Remember, though, that the most glorious words can sound dull and uninteresting. A singsong voice can turn the most beautiful poem into no more than a toothpaste jingle.

Select poems for your child with care. If you like a particular poem, chances are your child will too. Review the language and concepts in the poem and explain anything you think your child would not understand. Be sure he knows what is happening and who the characters are. Before you read the poem to him, read it through on your own. Phrase the words so they're meaningful. Think of how you could make your reading more exciting by using different voices, body pantomime, finger movements, pictures, or puppets. If possible, try to select a poem that relates to an event in your child's life, or has to do with the seasons, the weather, or anything else he might find interesting. A poem about the circus after he has seen it for the first time, an autumn poem when the leaves are changing, or a poem about the rain during a thundershower all suggest ways to make poetry more relevant. You can probably find some good poems to read from among the following suggestions:

Helen Barten, *Do You Know What I Know?* New York: Abelard-Schuman, 1970.

Alice Gilbert, *Poems from Sharon's Lunchbox.* New York: Delacorte Press, 1972.

David McCord, *Every Time I Climb a Tree.* Boston: Little Brown & Co., 1967.

Poetry for Summer. Selected by Leland B. Jacobs. New Canaan, Connecticut: Garrard Publishing Company, 1970.

Poetry on Wheels. Selected by Lee Bennett Hopkins. New Canaan, Connecticut: Garrard Publishing Company, 1974.

Ennis Rees, *Tiny Tall Tales.* New York: Abelard-Schuman, 1967.

Zoo! A Book of Poems. Selected by Lee Bennett Hopkins. New York: Crown Publishers, Inc., 1971.

Library Visits

Now is the time to begin regular visits to the library, which your child soon realizes is a special place. In the children's room, allow plenty of time to browse. Perhaps the librarian can show your child where the books for his age are located. Since the vast array of books might be confusing to him at first, help him select a few books to take home. He may even see some of his own books at the library.

Many libraries have a story hour or films for young children. These experiences are a marvelous source of language stimulation. Through them, your child also learns to listen and react to another adult. After the story hour, he can tell you about something he did all by himself.

Using Music

Your three-year-old learns songs from records, radio and television programs. Don't be surprised to hear him sing the song from a soap or cereal commercial since those jingles are designed to be appealing and easy to learn. Your child might also enjoy having a radio in his room so he can listen to different kinds of music.

Records are cherished possessions to a three-year-old. Add to your child's collection as his interests broaden. Perhaps some of the following will catch his fancy:

Children's Sing-a-Long, Merry Records, MR 6006.

Davy Crockett and Other Western Favorites, Happy-Time Records, HT 1022.

The Day the Orchestra Played, Golden Records, LP 258.

50 Happy Years of Disney Favorites, Disneyland Records, STER-3513.

It's Roundup Time, Peter Rabbit Records, K-10.

Kiddie Hootenanny, Happy-Time Records, HT 1025.

The Little Engine That Could, Golden Records, LP 193.

Mairzy Doats and Other Fun Songs, Happy-Time Records, HT 1036.

Mary Poppins, Disneyland Records, ST 3922.

Puff the Magic Dragon, Golden Records, LP 149.

Sing-a-Long for Children, Vol. I, Happy-Time Records, HT 1005.

Sing-a-Long for Children, Vol. II, Happy-Time Records, HT 1016.

Using Colors

By now, your child may have strong color preferences. Encourage him to use color words. Ask him his "favorite color" and tell him yours. Whenever it's convenient, include colors in your conversation. For example, ask your child which he would like, the red glass, the blue hat, or the green towel. "Color" games also increase your child's familiarity with words for colors.

What Color Is Missing? is fun for three-year-olds. Show your child two blocks of different colors. Ask him to turn around and then remove one of the blocks. He must say which one is missing. Increase the number of blocks when you feel he's ready.

Color Riddles is another color-guessing game children enjoy. Give color clues: "I see something in the room that's green. What is it?" If more help is needed, you might add other information, such as: "We sit on it." As his language develops, your child can also ask the questions. A variation of this game can be played with old magazines. Show your child a picture of something orange. Ask him to find other pictures of orange objects in the magazine and to cut them out. Later, these pictures can be assembled in a scrapbook.

Using Numbers

Help your child expand his concepts of numbers by using numbers and words related to them in conversation: "There are *four* books on the table." "Bring me a *pair* of socks." "Let's *count* the dolls in your carriage." As you use these words in a natural way, their meaning becomes apparent to your child. He will appreciate their usefulness in helping convey his thoughts more precisely.

Using Social Experiences

Most three-year-olds are mature enough for organized situations with other children. These may be in nursery school, scheduled play groups, pre-kindergarten classes, or specialized art, dance, gym, or music classes. If you haven't discovered any of these by yourself, use the best source of all: other mothers. You can also call your local school, "Y," church, or temple. Classified ads in newspapers or notices in supermarkets and neighborhood stores can also provide suggestions.

Social experiences are excellent for language enrichment because your child develops the ability to talk to a variety of people. He learns to deal with individuals beyond his immediate family and circle of friends, learns their expressions, and is forced to make himself understood. As he moves into new situations, your child discovers how to cope with new experiences. His confidence in his ability to handle new people and events increases dramatically at this stage. The child who clung fearfully to your hand on the first day of nursery school is soon transformed into the confident "plant waterer" at "my school."

The benefits in terms of language growth from these kinds of activities are noticeable. Your child has many new topics for conversation, and through the experiences he has with others, he begins to develop interests that, in turn, stimulate further language.

Community Experiences

Your child learns new language by visiting different places. At the same time he gains new topics for conversation as well as a great deal of information to share.

A trip to a museum when there is an appropriate exhibit can provide much learning. Some cities have museums of natural history that show ancient animals as well as the habitat of animals alive today. Perhaps there is an art museum with a "Please Touch Me" exhibit for children. You should also participate in any parades or celebrations in your town. Your three-year-old senses the excitement of these special events and can become involved. Return to places you may have visited when he was younger. You'll notice he responds differently now and delights in remembering past visits to the zoo, pet store, or beach. He may be motivated to share these past and present experiences with his nursery school class or friends.

Some excursions during this year may be without you. His class may visit the fire station, or a friend's mother may take him to the puppet show in the park. Then you become his audience. By asking questions, you help your child put his impressions into words. Listen patiently as he tells you what happened and how he felt about it. Don't interrupt to correct facts or add details; allow him to interpret experiences in his own way. Children, as well as adults, vary in their approach to a situation and in the aspects they find meaningful. Allow your child as much freedom as possible to deal with the world according to the way his personality dictates.

ADVANCED ACTIVITIES

*Sequence

Your child is beginning to understand the concept of
continuity and sequential order now—that events have a
beginning, middle, and end. The idea that certain things
happen before others becomes firmly established. You
can strengthen this idea of sequence and show him how
to organize his thoughts.

Arrange the Pictures

Cut out the pictures in a familiar storybook. Then help
your child arrange the pictures in the order of the events
in the story. Start with two or three pictures and gradually add more. For example, show him a picture of Cinderella dancing at the ball and one of her trying on the
glass slipper. Ask which picture came first in the story.
Your child probably knows Cinderella lost her slipper
when she left the ball and that she tried it on when the
prince came to her house the next day. Then you might
add a picture of Cinderella with her fairy godmother and
a picture of the stepsisters getting dressed for the ball.
Ask your child to put these in the correct order. After he
has assembled the pictures, ask him to tell the story.

Story Board

Assembling a story board is another way to help your
child understand sequence. Draw several pictures of
something unfolding. You can show how a flower grows
by finding or drawing pictures of a seed, a shoot, a bud,

and the full blossom. After shuffling the pictures, ask your child to arrange them in the correct order. Another story board could illustrate the building of a block tower. Show the box of blocks, the building of the tower in progress, and maybe a jumble of blocks after the tower has been knocked down. A familiar experience, like a birthday party, also makes a good story board. Writing the invitations, baking the birthday cake, greeting the guests, playing games, and opening presents are some picture suggestions for that topic. While your child arranges the pictures, talk about what they illustrate and discuss other possible arrangements.

Calendar

Record your child's appointments, dates with friends, classes, special visits, and any other events on a calendar. Using a calendar this way teaches your child the days of the week and helps him visualize and talk about the concepts of yesterday, today, and tomorrow. It also helps him develop a sight vocabulary. When he sees the word "art" on his calendar every Tuesday, for example, he'll soon recognize it as being the same word as the one on the door of the art room. If the calendar shows your child when a special event or favorite class is going to take place, he can understand why he must wait. He can also anticipate events more accurately if he knows when they're going to occur in relation to the rest of his schedule. Another advantage for a child in having his own calendar with his special dates is that it makes him feel more grown-up.

Discuss plans with your child and begin to ask his opinion about the more flexible parts of your schedule: "Would you rather visit Timmy today or tomorrow?"

"Should we go to the library now or after lunch?" By
consulting your child in advance, you're showing your
consideration for his opinions while encouraging him to
use language. Attitudes that increase your three-year-
old's feelings of competency and self-worth are a valuable part of your relationship.

*Sounds

High and Low teaches your child to identify the pitch of
sounds. Demonstrate the difference between a high
sound and a low one, using a piano, bells, pitch pipe,
gongs, or your own voice. Make two sounds and ask your
child to guess which was the high one and which the low.
Start with sounds that are far apart on the scale and
gradually move them closer to one another.

When your child can successfully make this type of
discrimination, ask him to respond to a series of notes by
standing up tall if the sound is very high, and crouching
closer to the floor as the pitch drops. The variations in
pitch can be subtle or more obvious depending on your
child's ability. Your three-year-old also enjoys playing
the notes for you or producing different sounds with his
voice.

Judging Sounds develops a critical appreciation of
sounds. Explain the difference between a sound that's
pleasing and one that's disagreeable to the ear. Ask your
child for examples of sounds he likes to hear and those
he doesn't enjoy listening to. If he has difficulty thinking
of something, ask him to categorize such sounds as
laughing, crying, sneezing, coughing, the screech of a
car's brakes, the clock ticking, water running, singing, a
typewriter, or any other sound he might know.

8.
The Age of Reason: Four to Five Years

Increasing self-reliance and an ability to adapt to a widening variety of situations characterize this age. Your four-year-old is just about ready to take on the world. His life gains in stability as he learns to interpret the zigs and zags of everyday events. He's enthusiastic about everything that happens around him and receptive to every fresh opportunity. Little escapes his notice.

It's an age of experimentation, of zest for living. Your child continually tests his parents and his home and social environment to determine the outer limits of acceptable behavior. He's willing to try anything, but still requires your support in any new ventures and your firm, adult guidelines. Now's the time to encourage him to button his own shirt, help clear the dinner dishes from the table, drip-dry the doll's clothing. But he must also be led to understand there are things he can't attempt yet. Crossing the street alone is still too risky, and as for transporting the steaming roast from oven to dining room, he'd better let Mother handle it a bit longer.

A strong sense of his own identity now emerges as he

reacts to his experiences. Experimentation with different behaviors forms a foundation for his unique personality. Your child learns when to take chances and when to play things safe. He's subject to moods: Sometimes he relishes company, other times he'd rather be left on his own. His discovering just what he prefers doing on his own and what he wants others to do for him contributes to his personality development.

Your four-year-old recognizes his kinship with others in his age group. In play, he becomes more sensitive to the ego needs of his pals. Sharing playthings and taking fair turns become accepted practice as he realizes that such behavior smooths the flow of social interaction.

With the increasing influence that his friends have over him, peer pressure becomes a factor he must learn to reckon with. When Ricky saw how easily Jordan could zip up his own jacket, he quickly was motivated to learn "the trick" himself. Suzanne has been trying for weeks to snap her fingers with the same ease as her friend Eileen. Rona is trying her hardest to roller-skate as smoothly as Amanda, an incipient champion.

Your four-year-old should be able to tend to most of his physical needs. Putting on his mittens, scrubbing his face, brushing his teeth, going to the bathroom are activities he now accomplishes independently. His physical energies and agility are by now quite impressive and they allow him a wide measure of freedom. Indeed, some of the daredevil feats he may now perform in the playground or backyard can make you shudder. He also has finer control of his hands now. He can use crayons, markers, paint and brush—and should be able to cut much more than a caper with a pair of blunt children's scissors. Each newly acquired physical skill enhances your child's feeling of competency.

At the same time, his ability to think logically and rationally is refined, though he'll still need your help in interpreting certain bewildering events. Scott was watching television when a news flash interrupted the show to report an airplane crash. Scott was transfixed as he listened.

Somewhat breathless and still shaken, he went to tell his mother about the bulletin. She explained the realities of such incidents in language he was able to absorb, then patiently answered his questions about plane crashes. The child was particularly upset because he knew that his father often used airlines for business travels. His mother tried to help him comprehend that plane accidents were rare. She was trying, above all, to calm his fears, to put the shattering newscast into terms with which he could deal. Nevertheless, the incident left its mark on Scott for some time. He'd reenact the crash with his own fleet of toy planes, and often during the next weeks, would ask his father some hard questions about his business flights. Largely due to the intelligent information his parents so willingly provided, his obsession with the subject faded away in time.

Language in the Child's Expanding World

Your relationship with your four-year-old changes subtly as he starts spending more time away from you. Until this age, the family has been the major source of language stimulation, but by four, most children regularly engage in away-from-home activities. Visits and even overnight stays with friends become more frequent. Nursery school, play groups, and other organized children's activities occupy many hours of a four-year-old's day. What has your little stranger been up to while out of your sight? More and more, you have to rely on his own *verbal* reports to find out.

Joey's nursery school went to visit an ice cream plant.

Joey shared the day's sublime activity with his family at the evening mealtime reunion. He described all the mouth-watering ingredients—the fruits and nuts, the creams, beans, and chocolate chips—that went into the manufacture of frozen treats. But he also shared the uniquely personal experiences of his field trip. There was the proud moment when teacher selected him to distribute the box lunches, the luscious taste of the ice cream samples, the pain when a can of fruit juice fell on his toe, his disappointment that he wasn't able to share a seat with his best friend on the bus trip home. In this world they no longer fully participated in, Joey's parents realized how dependent they were on their son's candor to learn about his feelings and impressions.

Your child may prove reluctant to share some aspects of his newly acquired private life. His nagging fears about sleeping at his friend's house without benefit of a night light, his intense desire to run faster than a pal— these are typical "secrets" he may not care to reveal. Instead of subjecting him to any kind of "third degree," respect such private feelings. Let your child describe his feelings in his own way, in his own good time. It's essential that you accept whatever he chooses to tell you, but at the same time become attuned to the underlying meaning of his words. In time, you may learn to gather a lot of significant impressions both from what he says and from what he doesn't say.

Children can be infinitely subtle. When something "bugs" them, they may conceal it in various artful ways during their conversations with you, rather than blurting it out directly. When Carol's father started a new business venture, her mother seemed (at least in Carol's judgment) to be spending an awful lot of time giving him a helping hand. When she wasn't in nursery school, Carol found herself being shunted off somewhere to stay with friends or to take part in group play. She never openly objected to these new arrangements, but soon her mother sensed that something was troubling her daughter. She listened more closely than ever to what Carol had to say, and began to ponder the changes she'd noticed in her behavior. These days, Carol seemed to be growing more and more dependent. Often now, her mother would hear, "Help me, Mommy!" Carol even seemed to be "unlearning" many of the things she really knew how to do for herself.

When her mother grasped the problem and its cause, she retailored her work schedule to allow her to spend more time with her daughter. She also took the trouble to explain why certain periods of separation were now unavoidable. On a few occasions, she took Carol along to the office. Carol appreciated all this special attention —and was now able to make a rapid adjustment to the changed circumstances of her life.

Patterns of Language

The depth and complexity of your four-year-old's language will amaze you. It's so vastly different from that of the three-year-old! Not only is it more elaborate, but it now incorporates slang and voguish new words along with your own pet expressions, clichés, and even some uninspired hyperbole. You'll hear your four-year-old mouthing phrases right out of television and from salty disc jockeys. Some of this lingo may even stymie you.

While your child is now well on his way to mastering most of the mechanics of language, errors in speech sounds, grammar, and sentence structure naturally persist. Nevertheless, he's now aware of many of the "rules" of good speech, and may even spontaneously correct himself. He's also beginning to develop some control over the timbre and tone of his voice.

Regional traits begin to appear in your child's speech at this age. The characteristic pronunciation and rhythms of a midwestern, southern, or New England accent may become noticeable. A four-year-old is also more aware of other people's speech. When he hears someone with an alien accent or a different speech pattern than his own, he's almost sure to comment on it.

Language Is a Game

Silly words and nonsense syllables, unnatural sounds and rollicking rhymes—all these can provide heaps of fun, especially for the four-year-old. Jokes, japes, and riddles are part of his repertoire, and it's not uncommon for him to inject a bit of gibberish or patter in the midst of more conventional language. What you hear is quite different from the jargon used by the eighteen-month-old trying to imitate his mother's speech. The four-year-old is perfectly capable of speaking intelligibly, but, in his natural exuberance, he seems to delight in letting go and talking silly.

"I'm going to the gee-gee on my poo-poo," he exclaims, though he could jolly well tell you where he's going in more civilized terms. Parents should treat this kind of giddy talk with indulgence. Your child is simply expressing his sense of humor.

Naughty words still fascinate a child at this stage. Having picked them up from peers or from adults, he may enjoy repeating them endlessly. If the words annoy you, explain that they don't sound very appealing, that you don't enjoy hearing them. Try to monitor the language your child hears at home or when he's with friends, but otherwise don't make a big fuss over the matter. Some experimenting with offensive words is inevitable, especially since today the air seems saturated with them. Just don't let the issue lead to a major conflict. After you've asked your child not to use certain words, try to overlook any slips—intentional or otherwise. A calm attitude on your part can be very helpful in discouraging the use of such words.

Conversation, Juvenile-Style

Although your child at this stage still understands more language than he employs, he can by now hold his own in a conversation. Take advantage of his eagerness to talk about everything and anything to establish solid lines of communication. Broaden your discussions by asking relevant questions.

During a nature walk with her class, Melissa stumbled upon a beautiful stone. With great pride, she displayed her treasure to her mother. Instead of greeting the find with a perfunctory "That's nice," Melissa's mother shared her daughter's enthusiasm, then asked questions that stimulated a conversation: "Where did you find that wonderful stone?" "What does it remind you of?" "What do you think we might use it for?" Your child is quick to gauge your interest in what he has to say. He appreciates your willingness to spend some time talking with him about subjects dear to his heart.

Living with Fantasyland

At this age, a child is given to flights of fancy and to some stretching of the truth. He understands that he has the

power to say both what's truthful as well as what's con-
cocted out of his imagination. Sometimes it becomes
difficult for him to make the distinction between things
as they are and as he'd like them to be. He may begin by
exaggerating facts and wind up light-years from reality.

Use language to help your child distinguish fact from
fantasy. If you hear him brag that his cat, Frosty, can leap
to the top of a tall building, you might discuss all the high
places he really can reach. "I've seen Frosty jump up to
the kitchen counter," you might tell him, "and once he
managed to leap onto Daddy's dresser." Then, introduce a note of skepticism about Frosty's supposed prow-
ess: "I don't think your cat could ever manage to reach
the roof of the garage, though. No, that's much too high
for him to spring." Try not to directly contradict your
child's wildest claims. He's simply testing the limits of
reality rather than deliberately misrepresenting facts.

Alibi-itis

As it dawns on him that not everything he says need be
the truth, your child becomes adept at alibis and self-
serving rationalizations. Sometimes, it even suits his pur-
pose to tell an outright lie. Freddie had been warned
many times not to ride his tricycle in the house. One day,
the temptation proved too overwhelming. Freddie decided there was ample time to try a few turns around the
living room before his mother returned from the basement with the laundry. As he rounded a corner between
the sofa and the TV set, he knocked over a plant. At the
very next moment, his mother entered the room. While
she surveyed the damage, little Freddie's mind began to
race.

"I didn't do it," he said. "The dog jumped on the

plant. I saw it, Mommy." But the dog, Freddie's mother knew, had been in the basement with her. And now she set about teaching her son an important lesson. She explained that he had to learn that lying disturbed her far more than his failure to heed her warning against bicycle riding indoors. Of course, he shouldn't have disregarded her instructions on that subject. But that was no excuse for lying.

"Don't ever be afraid to tell me the truth—ever again," she added, instructing Freddie to put the tricycle back in the closet and to sweep up the scattered soil and plant-pot fragments.

Faced with the choice of punishing Freddie for the accident or using it to instill values, Freddie's mother had decided on the latter course. She taught her son that she'd rather he tell "the awful truth" than try to placate her with a lie. Whatever your attitudes may be on moral issues, language is an effective vehicle for communicating them to your child.

Imaginary Companions

A four-year-old's world may include make-believe friends and mythical places. An invisible companion may keep him from being fearful and alone when his room is plunged into darkness or there's no one at hand to play with. He may enjoy long conversations with these pretend-folk and may refer to them in later talks with real audiences.

Chatting with unreal pets and pals allows your child to practice social skills. Don't challenge him about these relationships. He knows quite well that they only exist in his own mind, but their use as sounding boards satisfies important psychological needs. As he grows older, a child's imaginary friends should depart gracefully. Still, parents should be sure that their children have sufficient contact with three-dimensional friends and enough concrete activities to keep them busily involved.

A Quest for Answers

By now, your child has learned to impose a degree of censorship over what he chooses to say. He knows now that it isn't polite to say someone is funny-looking, but he won't hesitate to question you about why a certain person's face is so strange. He learns to be more careful about the statements he makes before learning to exercise the same degree of discrimination with regard to his questions. It seems that your four-year-old feels responsible for his direct statements while sensing that his inquiries permit him greater freedom. Thus, questions increasingly become the windows through which you can view your child's mind.

Kim met a child at nursery school whose parents were recently divorced. The parents had separated, Kim was told by her friend, because they were always fighting and had stopped loving each other. Now the father no longer lived at home; the child could only visit him at specified times. Kim was confused by all she'd learned about this "broken" family. One day when she heard her own parents quarreling over some small matter, she wondered, had they too fallen out of love? Were they about to divorce? She began to bombard her mother with odd questions. Would her father be obliged to go off to live in a hotel? Would she only be able to see him on weekends?

Kim's parents were concerned over the content of their daughter's queries, for Kim had never confided her newly acquired half-knowledge about divorce nor the fears that she was experiencing. Her feelings were translated into questions because she hadn't dared bring up the subject directly.

During a conference with her nursery school teacher, Kim's parents learned the real source of her questions. Then they were able to deal with Kim's apprehensions in a straightforward way. They explained to her why married people sometimes separate and, of course, reassured her about the state of their own marriage.

At this age, nothing is too small or petty to escape your child's attention. His questions become increasingly specific and focus on many sides of a subject. As Lauren watched a worm squirming across the grass, she began to study it with beady-eyed intensity. It was surely not the first time she'd encountered a worm, but her newly acquired verbal and intellectual skills now permitted her to express her curiosity as never before. Her probing questions reflected this ability to observe detail: "How does a worm pick up his food?" she asked. "How does he take a bath?" "How does a worm breathe underground?" "Where does a worm sleep?" and "Does the sidewalk scratch his stomach when he crawls over it?" A four-year-old's mind is a most inquisitive instrument.

Language serves an important function in helping your four-year-old organize his life, in allowing him to conceptualize his ever-broadening environment. Not surprisingly, he wants to know when certain things are going to happen: "When am I going to have my dinner?" "When is Julie's birthday party?" "When is Daddy coming home?" "When is Halloween?" When? When? When?

If you think many of your four-year-old's questions are unreasonable, consider that you too would be firing a barrage of questions if you found it necessary to function in a new, unfamiliar environment. Imagine yourself suddenly transported to a computer center. Probably, the more you noticed about the place, the more practical knowledge you'd try to elicit from the informed personnel there. At first your questions would be fairly general, but as your familiarity with how things functioned increased, they'd become more specific. Until you understood how every knob and relay operated, your questions would very likely tumble forth in rapid-fire, relentless, four-year-old fashion. Your child, during his early years, finds himself in somewhat the same situation —a stranger in a world he never made. The more his questions are answered, the more confidence he gains in his ability to deal with the unknown, the unforeseeable, the unexpected.

What really matters most are not your child's questions so much as your responses to them. In your attitude to his inquiries, you acknowledge (or fail to acknowledge) your child's importance in your own life. When your answers are consistently supportive, informative, and kindly, your child gets to feel that what he says is of value. Above all, answer his questions with honesty. Don't, out of ignorance or sloth, offer your child any misinformation that you'll later have to retract. Your skirting the truth only erodes the trust he places in you. Truthful answers insure your credibility.

In short, your discussions provide your child with invaluable material; he gets not just the information he may seek, but a feeling of self-worth, an ability to perform with competence, and the self-confidence he needs to expand both his mind and his experiences. A child's questions are a direct appeal and an instant mode of communication. Welcome his questions—they indicate a lively mind and an active curiosity.

Language—and Growing Social Awareness

At four, language is an important part of playtime with friends. Instead of grabbing for his neighbor's toy, a child of this age can negotiate an exchange. Conversations between four-year-olds tend to warm the heart of a listening adult. The children barter information, exchange experiences, plot, debate, argue, or agree with the utmost seriousness and intensity, tinged with a kind of innocence that soon will vanish forever. How methodical they are when they plan ahead, blocking out time for each activity or game! How charmingly organized they appear when, by mutual consent, they put aside the pail and shovels to take up their toy trucks. Construction time is over for the afternoon; now make way for the cross-country trailers. Four-year-olds need less adult guidance in their play or their talk. Language helps them to make things run smoothly.

You can help your child establish rapport with strangers and "new people." He'll have to learn to relate to many kinds of people in his lifetime and use his social skills in many new, unexpected situations. As preparation, encourage your child to use language now anytime the opportunity arises. Allow him to voice his opinions, to ask questions, to relate to other people independently.

Visits to the shoe store were always an ordeal for Wendy's mother because her daughter never liked to be kept waiting. She decided that the next time Wendy needed a new pair of sandals, she'd let her run the whole show. First, she allowed the child to choose when they ought to shop—whether it should be first thing in the morning or just after lunch. Then, while they waited to be served, Wendy (with her mother's guidance) was allowed to choose several styles of sandals from the display rack.

When their turn came, it was Wendy herself who asked the salesman to measure her foot size. She indicated the shoe styles she preferred, and asked him to bring them in her size. After trying on two pairs, Wendy told her mother which felt more comfortable; this was the pair she wanted to buy. Wendy's mother gave her the cash to pay for her purchase, and Wendy proudly carried her package home. An active, independent participant in this shopping expedition, Wendy learned the language and behavior appropriate to the situation. She also developed the confidence to relate to others in a "grown-up" situation.

The handiest way of teaching your child social graces is through your example. If the words "please" and "thank you" are second nature to you, there's every reason to believe your child will make them part of his own vocabulary. Occasional reminders to be polite may be necessary, but if you find yourself constantly nagging, it may be time to evaluate your own behavior.

Manners, to be sure, are more than lip service and go beyond "please" and "thank you." A child exposed to bickering and rudeness quickly starts to ape these negative behavior patterns. He'll also overhear and be influenced by the way his parents gossip about other people when they're not there. Carping, criticizing parents tend to produce a rude, petulant child. On the other hand, a child with parents who view their peers with a measure of goodwill will probably adopt their tolerant attitude. Children pick up subtle biases and prejudices by listening to their parents. Though later observation and experience may modify one's original attitudes, early conditioning (good or bad) is difficult to overcome.

This is the age when your child becomes aware of the

ritual social events in life—and becomes curious about how they may involve him now or later. The marriage of a relative or friend is of absorbing interest. He wants to know all about the bride and the groom and the ceremonial wedding traditions. The birth of a baby, a graduation, a confirmation—all such special events intrigue him. Satisfy his curiosity about these happy occasions.

When your child expresses an interest in the subject of death, discuss it with him. On the way to visit his great-grandparents, four-year-old Kenny turned to his parents as the family approached their destination and said, "They must be very old. When are they going to die?" His parents were dumbfounded at this question, which expressed their son's awareness of the fragility of old age. Kenny's parents assured him that although his great-grandparents were indeed quite advanced in years, they remained in relatively good health. They also told him how fortunate he was in getting to know this unusually hardy pair of forebears.

Four-year-olds often express their fears of death through their questions. They may bluntly ask, "When are you going to die?" or "Am I ever going to die?" Such questions can be agonizingly hard for parents to answer, but do try to tackle them head-on. Avoid any explanations that might invite confusion or fright. If you tell your four-year-old that a person goes to sleep forever when he dies, he could well develop anxieties about falling asleep in his own little bed each night.

The language you use to respond to such questions actually reflects your own attitudes. Some parents choose to explain death away by saying the person who died has "passed away" or "is up in heaven" or perhaps "among the angels." Others prefer more straightforward language. However you handle the subject, make sure your language honestly reflects your own views.

With regard to family affairs, you must decide just how much you wish to confide in your child; this should depend on the extent of his interest and how mature he is. Try to be as truthful as possible when explanations are required. Probe your own feelings about any sensitive matters so that when your child springs a question you'll be prepared to answer him honestly and clearly.

Language and Intellectual Growth

Plunged into a complicated, not to say crazy, world, your child spends the rest of childhood sorting things out, developing his own perspectives on life. His questions, his observations, his trial-and-error behavior, all help him to learn about his environment. The more his language ability grows, the better able he is to use this precious tool to organize his perceptions.

You can help your child organize information about his world into meaningful categories. Through language, you enable him to form accurate concepts about his experiences, which will shape and order his thoughts. Concept development is directly dependent on language ability.

Show your child how language provides the most effective way of grasping impressions and grappling with one's surroundings. Use language to describe and to categorize sensations. "How does your tomato juice taste this morning?" you might ask. "Is it cold, warm, tepid, bitter, sweet, or sour?" "How does the cat's fur feel to your touch? Smooth, stringy, bristly, cuddly, moist or dry?" Encourage your child to use language to relate his feelings: "How do you feel when the time comes to leave the playground? Are you sad, angry, relieved, happy, resigned, or eager?"

Show him how language can be used to examine another's feelings: "How do you think Grandma feels when we come to visit her?" "What does Benjy think when you won't let him share your toys?" "How do you suppose Daddy feels when he comes home from work?"

Your child's vocabulary increases as he searches for the word that will tell you precisely what his reactions are. Maybe he'll decide that Grandma feels overjoyed, Benjy betrayed, and Daddy just plain pooped.

Your four-year-old is capable of rational thought: He gathers information and impressions, which he shapes into a kernel of knowledge based on his own interpretations. At times he's accurate; at other times he may be way off base.

Donny and his parents were about to take a vacation. For days before their departure, Donny played with his set of electric trains. "All aboard!" he exclaimed gleefully. "Choo, choo! We're passing a farm. Here comes a tunnel. Look at those high mountains. Now we're crossing a bridge." Donny's parents began to think he knew more about railroad travel than they did.

When the great day arrived, Donny was beside himself with excitement. At the railroad station he began to inspect everything—and then grew more and more upset. Finally, he asked, "Where is the box? I can't find it anywhere!" The box he was looking for was the rheostat he used in his home train set to control his toy engine's speed. Donny's parents explained how a real train worked and what the role of the engineer was. When at last the train arrived, they asked (and were granted) permission to allow their child to inspect the engine and watch the engineer at his controls.

Back in their coach seats, Donny's father gave his son a cram course on the operation of a real train. He included some fairly complex information on the working of a steam engine, switching and shunting of passenger trains and freights, the responsibilities of the engineer, grade crossings and banking, timetables and schedules. Some of his explanations were probably above Donny's head, but there was a considerable amount of data that the child was able to absorb. His trip thus proved not only visually stimulating, but also an occasion to gather valuable information.

Just as your child may not have grasped everything you told him when he was younger, there are things you may consider too complicated for him at this age. Still, it's essential that you continue to challenge and involve him, to allow his intellectual capacities to "overreach." If you think some idea or thought is not coming across to him, repeat it in somewhat different language. You'll be amazed how much information your child yearns to have and put to use. So next time you're tempted to put down your child's question with "I think you're too young to understand," take the time, instead, to break down the correct answer into easy components. Some of the most difficult concepts can be readily simplified, if you'll make the effort.

Your four-year-old is now well on the way to understanding the concept of time in relation to the events in his life. Life, he perceives, is much more than the happenings of the moment. Yesterday it rained and he recited his poem in class without a flaw. Tomorrow it may rain some more or the sun may shine, but he must remember to bring a bag of sugar to school for the cookies his class will be baking. That birthday party invitation for next Saturday is still many days off—and this sort of time concept he may be as puzzled about as ever. His constant demand, "When is next Saturday?" indicates his still hazy understanding of just how time is organized on adult calendars.

"Today is Wednesday," you repeat with patience (we hope), "tomorrow is Thursday, the next day is Friday, and then comes Saturday, the day of Roger's birthday party." Consulting a calendar together will help make the flight of time more concrete.

Language can help your child apportion his time intelligently. Just thirty minutes before it was time for her to leave for school, Jackie asked her mother if she might paint. There wasn't time enough, Jackie's mother explained, to set up the easel, paint a picture, and then clean up. She suggested that Jackie wait until she returned from school; there would be lots of time to paint before dinner. Meanwhile, she offered to read Jackie a story before they left for school. Jackie was learning to plan her time realistically, to understand that sufficient time must be allowed to complete a project.

To keep abreast of just what your child already understands and to learn what things still confuse him, try to listen to him carefully; then modify—gently and tactfully —any misconceptions he may have acquired. Children may long persist in holding on to misguided notions: Milk comes from paper cartons, soup is made in cans, and fruits sprout on supermarket shelves. To correct these ideas, be sure your child understands the chain of events involved in food production—reinforce your own descriptions with information from books and with illustrations; make an occasional trip to the country or to a home garden. When you're shopping, you might point out the differences between corn still in the husk and the kernels of corn that have been frozen or canned. You can go on from there, of course, and let your child in on the secrets of preparing creamed corn, succotash, or such exotica as "vegetables Hawaiian style."

The right word or phrase can do much to clear up a misconception or to help organize a set of facts. Alex had a few nebulous ideas about how and why it rains. He knew vaguely that water from the soil somehow went up to the sky, formed clouds, then fell again as rain. To expand their son's understanding of the rain phenomenon, Alex's parents decided to demonstrate the concept of evaporation.

They filled a tumbler with water, drew a mark at the top of the water line, then left the glass overnight on the kitchen counter. In the morning, when they checked the water level, Alex saw at once that it had fallen. His parents explained that the water had gone into the air in a process known as evaporation. Then they told him about condensation—the process in which water, in turn, is removed from the air. Alex learned a good deal of new language that day, and when the concepts of evaporation and condensation are taught to his class at school, he'll have a valuable head start.

Be alert to all such opportunities to increase your child's storehouse of knowledge. The rewards your efforts will reap are well worth the extra time and thought required. Your joint investigations and research will also stimulate your child's appetite for learning and encourage him to follow through on ideas needing clarification.

Language in Decision-Making

You can use language in many ways to help your child develop confidence in his own judgment. Let him express his opinions openly. Never put a child's opinions down or suggest that they may not measure up. Refer to them whenever possible; your four-year-old will be delighted to find he has a voice in family life.

When Silas's family prepared to buy a new car, there

was the "awesome" task of choosing just the right color. Silas's father covered the living room table with paint chips and asked each member of the family—including Silas—to express his preference. The choice was finally narrowed down to "Sea Mist" or "Burnt Bronze." Silas's parents felt that either shade would be acceptable, so they allowed little Silas to make the final decision. After much deliberation and inner debate he revealed his choice: It would be "Burnt Bronze." The day the car arrived, Silas made sure everyone in the neighborhood understood that it was he who'd chosen the color. His self-esteem had received a big boost through this experience.

Instill in your child the courage to make his own decisions—and accept the inevitable risks. An independent, resourceful spirit is a precious asset in life. You might let your four-year-old help choose his friends' birthday gifts. If some of his decisions backfire, help him cope with the disappointment. Maybe he'll have selected some toy that his friend already owns. Show him there's no need to be flustered: "Let's simply return the toy to the store. Now that we've seen all of Joel's gifts, we can exchange it for one he doesn't already have."

As long as he's given the opportunity to act on his own, your child soon learns to talk out disappointments and overcome frustrations. Language helps a child to reach reasoned decisions and to accept, or overcome, any less-than-successful consequences of his decisions.

Language and Creativity

Creativity is a rather elusive commodity. We all recognize creatively gifted children or adults—and we admire their accomplishments. Creativity, however, is present in everyone in varying degrees. When your child pretends he's a fireman or plays with a mythical friend, he's using his imagination. During this year, your child's increased language ability can help shape his budding creativity. Language expresses his inventiveness.

If you respect your child's original ideas and encourage him to follow through on them without flagging, his creativity is bound to flourish. Squelching his suggestions, on the other hand, diminishes his potential for original thought.

Valerie came home one day with a feather she'd captured in the park. While playing with it, she was struck by its resemblance to a paintbrush. She asked her mother if she might try to paint with it, then set to work at once with her paints, paper, and improvised brush. Well, the feather wasn't precisely a paintbrush, but Valerie was enchanted by the unusual patterns she was able to create with it. Soon her pages were filled with colorful, and sometimes charming, abstracts.

Valerie's mother admired the afternoon's creations and told her daughter how feathers once were used as writing instruments. At once Valerie dipped the stick end of her feather into a jar of blue paint and attempted to write her name. By this time, the feather had become fairly bedraggled so that the results were not phenomenally successful. Undaunted, Valerie now decided she'd use the color-splashed feather as an ornament. She stuck it into her pigtail and began to perform an Indian dance about the dining-room table. Although a hair wash was next on the schedule, Valerie had been given the opportunity to explore her own ideas freely and without restraint.

An open and inquiring mind is essential for developing language and creativity, and if your child is receptive to new experiences, his life can become challenging and fun. A four-year-old wants to probe the mysteries of phenomena that most jaded adults simply take for granted. By sharing your child's interest in life's minutiae, you can rejuvenate yourself. Take the time to marvel at a rainbow, to watch the goldfish swimming with such grace, to investigate the man-made miracle of a construction project, to talk about the way a baby learns to walk.

Let a little fantasy and a lot of humor enter into your relationship with your child. A few "tall tales" can safely be exchanged during your conversations—they add zest and stimulate your child's imagination. Spend some time with him pretending you live in a different part of the world. Make believe with him that his poodle is indeed endowed with the powers of human speech. Your child isn't likely to confuse pretense with reality, so go to it— share his language games.

Although suggestions may flow spontaneously from your child, you can use language to help spark his imagination. The carton that contained the new washing machine was just the right size to convert into the toy house Felice had long dreamed about. When Felice's mother saw how imaginatively her daughter was using the empty box, she suggested a bit of interior decoration. "Do you think your new house could use a touch of color on the walls?" she asked. Felice eagerly agreed. "I'll get my crayons," she said, "and draw some pictures there."

Once Felice had executed her murals, her mother suggested some home furnishings. Felice decided her bath towel would make an excellent rug. Her blanket and pillow, along with a few favorite toys, completed the furnishings. Her mother's contributions had involved Felice in a rewarding project.

Your child appreciates your positive attitude toward his work; your praise encourages him to develop his original ideas. When he finishes a drawing, compliment him. Don't settle for an offhand, halfhearted "That's nice!" Say something specific about the little masterpiece: "I love the shade of blue you chose for the sky." Or, "Those flowers are so colorful, so lifelike." Or, "Looking at that picture makes me feel happy."

Your attitude toward your child's explorations influences his self-image. If you value his novel approach in acquiring a new skill, that appreciation immediately communicates itself to your child. Daring to break the mold of conformity is a sign of a lively intelligence, but develops only when a child is allowed to express himself freely. When his impulses are suppressed in an environment fraught with preconceptions and rigid limitations, he's obliged to try to overcome handicaps that may prove insurmountable. An atmosphere of freedom and encouragement is a vital feeding ground for your child's creative ambitions.

Keeping Up with Your Child

Language learning, as we said at the outset, is an ever-expanding process. Language grows and changes throughout childhood; the process, we hope, continues during your child's entire life. By the time your child reaches his fifth birthday, he has acquired most of the basic structure of language, but he still needs an accepting and stimulating language environment in which to practice his skills. As his mind and abilities develop, make every effort to keep up with him. Take into account his changing interests—and continue to contribute to the constant enrichment of his language.

Remember: Your role in helping your child not only to speak but to communicate, to gain self-confidence, and to relate to others is paramount. You should be as attentive to your five-year-old's language as you were when he said his first proud words, told you the happenings on his first day at nursery school, or made his first attempts to trick you with a riddle. The key is uncritical acceptance of your child's language efforts, and a devoted interest in them. There is still the occasional need for guidance and instruction now, which should take the form of establishing careful models he'll copy, issuing directions simple enough for him to follow, and offering frequent words of encouragement.

The methods and approach advanced in this book should equip parents to participate confidently in their child's language development. When followed, they provide a solid foundation for establishing lifelong communication. The games, conversations, and activities you share with your child express your pride and pleasure in him. Your participation as a partner in these precious and exciting years helps forge the links of love and trust that are essential for his growth as a wonderful human being.

ACTIVITIES

Better Ways to Listen

Your four-year-old's listening skills become more refined as he learns to appreciate the complexities of language. The ability to listen, concentrate, and remember is directly related to your child's future success in all areas of education.

Language Detective teaches your child to listen for verbal clues. Explain how an object can be identified by its characteristics. A ball is round; it bounces and rolls. Scissors are sharp; they cut and their parts move. You can also explain how the same word can describe properties shared by two objects. Both a doll and a chair have arms and legs. Sometimes, more information is needed to identify the object correctly. "Little children play with it" and "It's something we sit on" give additional information about the doll and the chair.

Think of an object in the room and give your child a clue: "I'm thinking of something that has hands." If he can't guess, give him another clue: "I'm thinking of something that has hands and numbers." If he still has difficulty, you might add: "I'm thinking of something that has hands, numbers, and tells us when to go to sleep." Perhaps you might have to say that the object tells us what time it is.

Make your clues more abstract as your child's skill increases. Allow him to give the hints to you. Try this game with objects that aren't in the room. Select items found in the supermarket, on a farm, or at the zoo.

"I Believe You" helps your child distinguish between fact and fantasy. Give him an example of a statement that's real and one that's pretend: "The boy can lift his bicycle" and "The boy can lift his Daddy's car." Tell him to show which statement he thinks is real and which one pretend by saying, "I believe you" or "I don't believe you." After a while, your four-year-old may be able to make up his own examples.

Vary this game by telling a story mixing fact and fantasy. When the story changes from real to make-believe, your child says, "I don't believe you." He must listen carefully for the transition: "Ivan had a beautiful gray cat named Silver. Ivan loved Silver very much. When Ivan went to sleep, Silver curled up at the end of the bed and

slept there all night. Ivan took very good care of Silver.
He gave his cat fresh food and water twice a day. Ivan and
Silver shared a secret. Silver could talk to Ivan and told
him stories late at night."

At this point, your child should say, "I don't believe
you." If he misses the clue, stop and tell him that something you've already said is make-believe. Review the
story and help him determine what wasn't true. Use
Aesop's fables or any other story your child hasn't heard
before to supplement your original material.

Story Questions teaches your child to listen for details.
Tell a brief story that has many facts: "The little girl went
for a walk with her father on a sunny afternoon. They
passed the library and the fire station. At the ice cream
store, he bought her a chocolate cone. The little girl
was very happy and thanked her father for the special
treat."

Ask your child questions based on the facts in the
story: "Where did the little girl go?" "What did they
pass?" "Where did they stop?" "What was the little girl's
special treat?" "How did the little girl feel?" "What did
she say to her father?"

Vary the number and complexity of the questions according to your child's ability. Perhaps you might choose
two or three of those sample questions at first. As your
child becomes more proficient, increase the difficulty of
the material to make the game more challenging.

"Sorry" helps your child learn to listen for content. Ask
him to bring you an object: "Bring me the cup." "Bring
me the book." Then tell him you're also going to ask for
some things that are impossible for him to carry: "Bring
me the door." "Bring me the piano." When you ask for
that type of item, he should say, "Sorry." Vary your
requests so that your child is encouraged to listen carefully: "Bring me the doll (fork, table, pencil, bed, couch,
paper, stove, television, or refrigerator)."

What Doesn't Belong? teaches your child to listen for the sentence that doesn't belong in a story. Tell a short story and include one sentence that's clearly out of place in the narration and ask your child to identify it: "Brian went out to play. His friend, Peter, had a new bat and ball. The boys played baseball. The farmer fed hay to the horses. Brian and Peter took turns hitting with the bat and pitching the ball. They were sorry when it was time to go home."

As your child's skill increases, make the sentence that doesn't belong less obvious: "Sharon and her family went on a car trip to visit her grandparents. They packed the car carefully. The family left early in the morning because they had a long trip. Sharon loves peanut butter. The trip took about four hours. Sharon and her parents played games in the car and watched the scenery. Her grandparents were very happy to see them."

If your child doesn't know the correct answer, review the story. Explain that since the story is about a car trip, whether or not Sharon likes peanut butter is irrelevant. This game also helps your child learn to be more concise when he tells a story.

Where Does It Come From? helps your child remember a story he's heard. Tell part of a familiar story: "The little girl carried the basket through the woods to her grandmother's house. She knew she wasn't supposed to speak to strangers." Your child should guess this excerpt comes from "Little Red Riding Hood."

Ask your child to guess where this portion of a story came from: "The boy's mother took the beans and threw them out the window. In the morning, there was an enormous stalk growing up into the clouds." He should answer, "Jack and the Beanstalk."

If your child can't guess, tell him a little more of the story. Possibly, he could give you an excerpt from his favorite story. Your four-year-old delights in trying to stump you.

Drawing Game teaches your child to listen carefully in order to follow directions. Give him a blank piece of paper and several crayons and tell him to follow your directions: "Draw a red line at the top of the paper. Put a green circle at the end of the line. Draw a blue square at the bottom of the paper." Your child enjoys watching the design take shape. Plan ahead so he ends up with a picture of an animal or some other recognizable figure.

Simple Simon, Giant Steps, and *Red Light–Green Light* are popular children's games that are also very effective in developing listening skills. Your child must listen for a particular word or combination of words in order to succeed in the game. Generally, more than one child participates. These games are fun to try when it's your turn to have the play group in your house or it's time for a birthday party.

Auditory Memory Games increase your child's ability to remember what he hears. In these games, your child remembers increasingly long lists. Start with "I'm going on a trip and I'm going to take my coat." Your child replies, "I'm going on a trip and I'm going to take my coat and pajamas [or anything else he'd like to suggest]." When it's your turn, repeat "coat and pajamas" and add another item. Each person repeats what was said before and adds one item, thereby lengthening the list.

When the packing-a-suitcase theme loses its appeal, change to, "I'm going to the supermarket, and I'm going to buy ———," or, "I'm having a party, and I'm going to invite ———," or, "I'm going to the toy store and I'm going to buy———." If your child has an idea for a theme, follow his suggestion. Soon you'll notice the increase in the number of items he can remember.

The song "Old MacDonald Had a Farm" can also be

used to improve auditory memory. Liberally praise your child's efforts at remembering, and stop the game if he gets frustrated because he can't remember more.

How to Encourage Reading

Since the skills of listening, speaking, reading, and writing are closely related, practice in one area has a positive influence on the others. Your child is probably aware of letters and may be able to identify certain ones. Some children, at this age, can also read words.

Your child's interest in learning to read develops as he's exposed to books, signs, labels, and certain television shows. At times he probably asks what a particular word says. You can help your four-year-old develop an awareness of sounds and the letters that represent them. The ability to recognize and differentiate individual sounds is invaluable in speech and reading.

The following activities are pre-reading games designed to help your child identify sounds and discriminate between them. These games use the sound when it comes at the beginning of the word, in the initial position (*m*ap). Then, after your child understands a sound in this position, use the same activities to teach the sound in the final (ha*m*) and medial (wo*m*an) positions in the word. Whenever possible, make each sound more concrete by referring to sound names—the "snake sound," the "buzzing sound," the "puffing sound," and so on.

Stop the game, which should be an exciting learning adventure, before your child gets bored or tired. He needs time to understand the new concepts of sounds, letters, and words.

Alphabet Sounds teaches that each letter of the alphabet has its own sound. You might start with the sound *m*.

Show your child pictures of words beginning with that sound: man, mitten, milk, monkey, moon, and mother. Say each word and ask your child to listen for the first sound he hears. Explain that each word starts with the sound *m*. Practice saying the words together. Talk about how the sound *m* looks, feels, and sounds. Show how the words for the pictures look when they're written and draw your child's attention to the letter *m* in the words. This game should be short and enjoyable. If your child's attention wanders, go on to a different activity.

On another day, you could introduce a new sound. You might choose the sound *p, t, s, f, l*, or any other consonant whose sound remains the same. Avoid using letters that have more than one sound, such as *c* in "cent" and "cat," and *g* in "go" and "giant." With these letters, the sound is pronounced differently in each word, and this could confuse a four-year-old.

Sounds Alike helps your child discriminate between sounds. After he's familiar with a particular sound, teach him to distinguish that sound from others. Tell him to listen for the sound *m* and to clap his hands when you say that sound in a series of sounds: *t, p, s, m, k, m, m, l, n, ch, m, m,* and *v*. Vary placement of the sound your child is trying to identify.

Then say a group of words and ask your child to clap when he hears a word that begins with the sound *m:* ball, map, see, hot, mat, tall, chair, big, man, meet, pan, march, and bench. Say the words naturally, without placing unusual emphasis on the initial sound. Asking your child to repeat the word he selects reinforces the sound for him. You might also show him a picture that illustrates his choice.

Pick-a-Word helps your child listen for the sound that's different. Give your child three words. Tell him that two of the words begin with the same sound and one begins with a different one. He must pick the word with the initial sound that differs from the others. Use sounds and words he knows, varying the position of the word you want him to select: ball, meet, boy/ go, tall, tree/ man, me, jump. When your child has shown he's able to pick the correct word, increase the number of words to four: see, pen, put, pail/ top, zoo, talk, tell.

Make a Scrapbook of Sounds

Ask your child to find pictures illustrating the words that begin with the sound he's learning. Old magazines, store catalogues, and his own drawings can be used. For example: for the sound *m* your child might select pictures of a man, the moon, a monkey, mittens, milk, and a mother. The sound *b* might be represented by a bathtub, ball, bench, button, boat, and bear. Let your child's imagination roam free, and you'll see that some of his suggestions may be quite original. Perhaps he could also try to find pictures that show feelings: a happy person for the sound *h*, a sad child who is crying for the sound *s*, or a tired person for the sound *t*. Pictures of actions are also good subjects for a scrapbook: children running for the sound *r*, a man mowing his lawn for the sound *m*, a lady swimming for the sound *s*. Label each picture and underline the sound it depicts.

How to Learn Categories

The first step in recognizing and forming categories is to match pictures or objects. After your child understands how to match identical things, broaden the category to include similar objects. In that way, he's asked to make more abstract judgments. Instead of matching only red balls, he now includes balls of other colors and sizes. Different types of shoes—from Daddy's loafers to Mommy's high heels—can go into the shoe category. The categories can be made even more abstract. A group of "all things that jump" could include children, kangaroos, and pogo sticks. "Living things" could depict people, plants, and animals.

Your four-year-old can also understand size groupings. Give him a collection of buttons to sort according to size and help him to pick the small, medium, and large ones. A group of different animals could also be arranged by size: The elephant and giraffe would go together in the "large" category, while the bird and mouse would be in the "small" category. The "medium" category might contain the monkey and dog.

How to Use Games

Four-year-olds are fledgling game players. They're old enough to understand rules and the importance of following them. If parents can get into the spirit of competition and fair play, these activities become as enjoyable for them as for their children. If the rules of a game are too difficult, adapt them for your child. However, once the rules are set, all players should follow them. Select games in which both you and your child can have success; don't always let him win. An element of luck in a game keeps everyone on his toes.

Many suitable commercial games don't require the ability to read. A knowledge of colors is an important element in some; others use matching skills or numbers. Lotto games teach matching and an appreciation of categories. Card games using pictures can be very exciting:

old maid, go fish, and concentration are popular with
four-year-olds. You can also make up your own games
using objects around the house, old magazines, and your
imagination.

How to Use Creative Dramatics

Begin dramatic play with short episodes from daily life.
A visit to the store to buy some groceries, a trip to the
dentist, or an experience as the juice monitor at nursery
school would all make good topics for creative dramatics. Briefly review what's going to happen and what you'll
talk about. A script is unnecessary because the essence
of creative dramatics is spontaneity. Some preparation
and familiarity with the subject, however, is essential. Let
your child's interests and ability determine the amount
of help you offer.

Creative dramatics also allows your child to leave the
familiar world behind and become whomever or whatever he'd like to be. Perhaps Goldilocks is your child's
heroine or the Gingerbread Man is more his style. With
a little assistance and planning, your four-year-old can
turn in a credible performance. Discuss the plot and the
characters' feelings and behavior, and decide on the kind
of voices to use:

"Why was Goldilocks in the forest?" "Where were the
bears?" "What did Goldilocks do in the bears' house?"
"How did the bears feel when they came home and saw
Goldilocks?" "What did they say?" "How could you
change your voice to sound like each bear?" "How did
Goldilocks feel when she saw the three bears?" "What
lesson did Goldilocks learn?"

"Who made the Gingerbread Man?" "Why did he run
away?" "Whom did he run away from?" "How could you

change your voice to sound like each character in the story?" "What finally happened to the Gingerbread Man?" "How was he fooled?"

Help your child with the stage directions and take a role yourself. Collect old hats, scarves, shoes, handbags, clothing, and other props for your theater. If you're relaxed, creative dramatics can be enjoyable and rewarding. It gives your child the opportunity to experience the lives and feelings of others—he learns to put himself in their place. Language growth is stimulated as your child discovers the many possible ways of expressing himself. He uses language from his daily life as well as from fairy tales, nursery rhymes, fables, and other stories. You may find that his friends would like to participate in this activity. If you'd like an audience for your performance, neighbors, siblings, and grandparents are ideal.

Using Puppets

Puppets are an exciting way to extend creative dramatics. Your child may feel more comfortable playing a role when he's acting through a puppet.

Make hand puppets from socks, paper bags, or sticks pasted on the backs of pictures. Construct a stage by using the edge of a table or a large carton. Plan simple stories. Nursery rhymes or other simple tales are a good source of material. "Jack and Jill" would make a charming puppet show. First discuss how the characters will behave and what kind of voice to use for each one: "Why were Jack and Jill going up the hill?" "What did they say to each other?" "How did they feel when they fell?" Chances are you'll be proud of your child's performance.

Puppetry is a wonderful means of artistic expression and can involve many creative skills. There are puppets

to make, the stage to construct, the story to write, the
dialogue to dramatize, and the show to produce. Older
children and adults also find puppetry a rewarding and
stimulating activity, and it can become a lifelong hobby.

How to Improve Voice Skills

Voice activities help your child control and improve his
voice by helping to make it a more flexible and effective
instrument.

Which Voice? teaches the concept of appropriate voice
volume. Discuss the difference between a quiet voice,
medium voice, and loud voice. Show your child pictures
of various settings: the library, playground, a restaurant,
nursery school classroom, and bedroom. Talk about the
voice volume that's right for each place. Give him examples of sentences he might say for each picture, using the
appropriate voice: "I want this book," in a quiet voice
(library). "I'm going on the slide," in a loud voice (playground). "I want spaghetti and meatballs for dinner," in
a medium voice (restaurant). "Can I paint, now?" in a
medium voice (nursery school classroom). "The baby is
sleeping," in a quiet voice (bedroom).

Ask your child to repeat the sentences using the appropriate voice volume with each one. Perhaps he could
suggest other sentences for those places. Talk about why
each voice is suitable and possible consequences of not
using the correct voice: The people in the library would
be disturbed if you used a loud voice; your friend in the
playground might not hear you if you used a quiet voice;
the baby in the bedroom might wake up if you used a
loud voice. Help your child develop the ability to select
and use the voice that best fits the circumstances.

Echo Game helps your child learn to control the volume

of his voice. Choose any word that appeals to him, such as his pet's name, a favorite toy, or the word "pizza." Stand close together and say the word in a quiet voice. Your child echoes the word. Then increase the distance between you and your child and raise the volume of your voice as you say the word. Use words at first and then whole sentences. Outside, this game can be played at even greater distances.

How Do You Feel? teaches your child how his voice communicates emotions. Talk about ways you can feel, such as cheerful, unhappy, angry, afraid, surprised, and worried. Explain that you're going to tell him how you feel through your voice. Say, "I feel so sad because I broke my favorite dish." Judging from the sound of your voice, your child says either, "Your voice sounds sad," or "Your voice doesn't sound sad." Try to make your voice as expressive as possible.

Let your child have an opportunity to use *his* voice to tell you how he feels. He may say, "I feel happy because I'm going to the circus." If you answer, "Your voice doesn't sound happy," explain how he could change his voice to show his feeling more clearly. Perhaps he spoke too slowly or too loudly. Maybe he could adjust his pitch. All these suggestions contribute to his mastering his voice and his ability to use this important instrument.

How to Use Books

Your four-year-old's curiosity is wide-ranging. Books can expand his interests and expose him to a large body of knowledge. If he's particularly fond of trains, show him how books help him learn all about them. At the same time, introduce new topics and ideas by taking advantage of the variety in children's literature. Peruse the book before you read it to your child. If you think the writing or content is not up to par, pass it by. Be selective about the books you choose for your child.

These early experiences with books can influence a child's attitude toward learning to read. If books have represented a rewarding way for him to spend time, reading becomes a skill he's anxious to acquire. Let your child see you read books, newspapers, and magazines. He'll learn that you like to read and that this activity is an important part of your life.Your four-year-old's command of language allows him to understand unusual words, characters, and stories. He appreciates unexpected rhymes, preposterous animals, or exaggerated situations. He's confident now of his ability to handle language and the concepts it represents. Help him learn to accept and understand different styles of writing.

Try many kinds of children's books. Perhaps your child would be interested in a picture dictionary, a book of riddles, or a book about science. Although a four-year-old still enjoys fairy tales and other classic children's stories, you are by no means limited to these books. Take advantage of the large selection of books at the library, of which the following list is only a small indication. Encourage your child to be adventurous.

Ben Ross Berenberg, *Golden Clock Book.* New York: Golden Press, 1976.

Francis Chrysler, *Riddle Me This.* New York: Henry Z. Walck, 1968.

Jean De Brunhoff, *The Travels of Babar.* New York: Random House, 1961.

Leonora and Arthur Hornblow, *Animals Do the Strangest Things.* New York: Random House, 1974.

John E. Johnson, *What's in the Dark?* New York: Parents' Magazine Press, 1971.

Iela and Enzo Mari, *The Apple and the Moth*. New
York: Pantheon, 1970.

Old MacDonald Had a Farm. New York: Grosset &
Dunlap, 1976.

Margaret and H. A. Rey, *Curious George Goes to the
Hospital*. Boston: Houghton Mifflin Company,
1966.

Richard Scarry, *Storybook Dictionary*. New York:
Golden Press, 1976.

Dr. Seuss, *If I Ran the Zoo*. New York: Random
House, 1950.

Dr. Seuss, *Horton Hatches the Egg*. New York: Random House, 1968.

Dr. Seuss and Roy Mekie, *My Book About Me*. New
York: Random House, 1969.

Shel Silverstein, *The Giving Tree*. New York: Harper
& Row, 1964.

John Steptoe, *My Special Best Words*. New York: Viking Press, 1975.

Ralph Underwood, *Ask Me Another Riddle*. New York:
Grosset & Dunlap, 1976.

Telling Stories Through Pictures

Your child learns to use his vocabulary more precisely as
he describes the events surrounding a picture. Show him
how he can start with a concrete set of facts, and then
interpret and extend them. Look at a pair of before and
after pictures such as a girl ice skating and the same girl
sitting on the ice crying. Ask your child to say which
picture happened first and then help him tell the whole
story, encouraging him to use his imagination to fill in
the missing details: "What did the girl trip on?" "Did she
hurt herself?" "Was she cold?" "Whom was she skating
with?" Another possibility is a set of pictures showing an

entire cake in one picture and half the cake gone in the
other. Ask your child: "Who ate the cake?" "Was the
cake for someone's birthday?" "How will the mother feel
when she sees the half-eaten cake?"

Try to find pictures for this activity in books, magazines, and among photographs. If you have difficulty
locating appropriate material, draw it yourself. Simple
stick figures will do just fine. The less detail you include,
the better, because your child must then use his own
resources to set the scene. Use events from real life if
something suitable occurs to you or create your own
episodes.

After your child is able to tell a story from a pair of
pictures, use just one. The picture you choose should be
fairly simple at the beginning, but can become more
complex as your child's skill increases. Initially, ask him
to describe what's happening in the picture at the time
portrayed. Later, he can tell you what he thinks happened before and after the event shown in the picture.
A picture of a group of children in a playground might
be good material. Ask your child to describe what he sees
in the picture. He can mention where the children are,
what games they're playing, and what kind of day it is.
Then, ask your child to tell you what happened before
the children came to the playground. Possibly, they ate
lunch, put on their jackets, and walked to the playground. After your child tells you everything he thinks
happened before, ask him what he imagines will happen
when the children leave the playground. He might say
they'll drink from the water fountain, walk home, and
then have a snack.

Perhaps your child could reconstruct the entire day
from the point of view of one child in the picture. Help
him tell you everything that happened to this child from
the time he woke up to the time he went to sleep. You'll

be delighted with your child's imagination and gain valuable insights into the workings of his mind in the process. The parts of his daily routine that he decides to include in the narration and those he chooses to omit can be revealing.

Many different subjects can be used for this activity. Eskimos in an igloo, animals in a forest, people working at their jobs, and elves living under a mushroom can all stimulate your child's imagination. Help him organize his ideas and select the ones to include in his story. Explain that some may not be needed because they're irrelevant to the main point of the picture.

Storytelling from pictures is a wonderful way to encourage language growth because it stimulates imagination and helps your child learn to express his thoughts and ideas clearly. Vocabulary development gets a boost as your child tries to find the right word to name the things he sees in the picture or to say something about it. He learns to look at a visual symbol carefully and interpret and refine it verbally. This skill is useful later when he learns to understand and use other visual symbols—letters—in reading.

How to Use Poetry

At this age poetry becomes another medium your child can use for entertainment and knowledge. Read poems that create a mood, tell a story, or make him laugh. Encourage your child to talk about how the poem made him feel or what it told him.

Your child's language is enriched when he's exposed to poetry. Help him recognize and appreciate unique or beautiful words and phrases as they occur in poetry. If he uses particularly imaginative language, compliment him. Show him how carefully chosen words are used to express a feeling or thought. The following books represent some of the different types of poetry for a child of this age.

> Roz Abisch, *Around the House That Jack Built.* New York: Parents' Magazine Press, 1972.
> Dorothy Aldis, *Favorite Poems of Dorothy Aldis.* New York: G. P. Putnam's Sons, 1970.
> Eleanor Farjeon, *Then There Were Three.* Philadelphia: J. B. Lippincott, 1942.
> John Lawrence, *Rabbit and Pork—Rhyming Talk.* New York: Thomas Y. Crowell Company, 1975.
> A. A. Milne, *When We Were Very Young.* New York: E. P. Dutton, 1927.

How to Use Music

Your four-year-old's record player and collection of records are very special to him. At times he likes to sing along with a favorite record or listen to a particular story over and over. At other times, he plays a record as background music when he's involved in another activity. Songs from radio and television shows also contribute to your child's interest in music.

A child of this age may become interested in a musical instrument if he knows someone who plays that instrument. At school, a teacher may play the piano or guitar as the class sings or dances. Concerts and ballets especially produced for young children can further develop your child's enjoyment of music. Exposure to a wide variety of musical experiences, some of which are represented in the following selection, promotes your child's appreciation and understanding of music.

Aesop's Fables, Golden Records, LP 152.

Alice in Wonderland, Peter Pan Records, BR 501.

Around the World in 80 Days, Happy-Time Records, HT 1051.

The Best of Gilbert & Sullivan, Merry Records, MR 6008.

Everybody Cries Sometimes, Activity Records, AR-561.

Free to Be . . . You and Me, Bell Records, 1110.

Great Children's Stories Told with Sound and Motion, MGM Records:

    Snow White, CH/CHS-501.

    Cinderella, CH/CHS-502.

    Pinocchio, CH/CHS-503.

    Bambi and Dumbo, CH/CHS-506.

    The Wizard of Oz, CH/CHS-510.

The Jungle Book Adventures of Mowgli, Happy-Time Records, HT 1052.

Peter and the Wolf, Golden Records, LP 154.

Pippi in the South Seas, G. G. Record Co., 6305-131.

Songs That Tickle Your Funny Bone, Golden Records, LP 197.

Time to Tell Time, Golden Records, LP 199.

How to Enrich Conversation

At this age, your child wants to tell you everything. Sometimes, his conversation combines fact and fantasy, and you'll find yourself listening to extremely inventive tales.

Since conversation is a two-way form of communication, ask questions, make observations, and comment on what your child has to tell you. This is an age of great verbal and mental experimentation, so sometimes it might be necessary to help your child organize and clarify his thoughts. Correct any misinformation or misunderstanding by gently and carefully providing accurate information without undermining self-confidence. It's very gratifying to have someone listen attentively to what we have to say. What a wonderful compliment you pay your child when he feels his conversation is valued!

Use conversations to expand your child's mind and to help him develop new perspectives on familiar facts. Ask your child to think of all the new things he could do with a simple object such as a pipe cleaner, a paper clip, the cardboard tube from the inside of a roll of paper towels, or the top of a spray can. He might also tell you what he would do if he could change places with you, his teacher, Batman, an astronaut, or a policeman.

Another interesting topic for conversation would be the way he might handle a particular situation: "How would you help Barbara learn to share her dolls?" "What would be a terrific new way to spend this afternoon?" "What would be a good idea for a Halloween costume?" Listen to his proposals and contribute your own ideas.

Your attitude determines how confident your child feels about expressing himself. Give your child the freedom to "think out loud"; he shouldn't feel he has to censor his thoughts first. If possible, follow through on actions or activities your child suggests.

Practice the art of conversation with your four-year-old—the skill he develops now will be of key importance throughout his life. Encourage him to use good manners during conversations: to listen to others and wait his turn. When others are speaking, he should learn to say, "Excuse me," if he must interrupt their conversation. Your child now begins to express mature insights and feelings, the forerunners of communication in later years.

How to Use Interests and Hobbies

Hobbies are a rich and fruitful part of life for children as well as adults. It's difficult to know whether stamp collecting, tennis, or the violin will ultimately be your child's major interest. However, the more varied his experiences are, the richer his language will be. A person with diversified interests is rarely bored or boring.

Experiences promote hobbies. A trip to the Museum of Natural History may awaken an interest in insects. A day in the park may lead eventually to a rock collection. A concert may develop a love of music, or an hour on ice skates may spark a desire to participate in the Olympics.

The natural tendency is to introduce your child to areas that interest you. This is a very positive course of action because your enthusiasm and joy are bound to be contagious. Perhaps there's something you've had a peripheral interest in, but have never had the chance to explore; now, you and your child can discover this whole new area together. If you've wanted to learn about shells, collect some at the beach and then get a library book to help you identify them. The shells can be used to make paperweights, frames, and planters. This new hobby of yours can also be a marvelous experience for your child since he learns how rewarding a faculty curiosity is.

How to Learn About Time

Your child's use and understanding of words to convey past, present, and future is becoming abundant. The day's events seem to be ordered fairly accurately. He knows when things usually happen, but may be uncertain about how long something takes and ask how many minutes he must wait until dinner will be ready or a friend

comes to play. Show your child different types of clocks.
A digital clock can make time more concrete for a child
this age.

Your four-year-old becomes interested in his own
past. He wants to know how he looked and acted as a
baby. Old photographs are a good introduction to the
past; he delights in seeing himself as an infant and toddler. Pictures of Mommy and Daddy as children, or as
bride and groom, are always popular. Discussions about
these pictures or about events your child remembers
help him feel part of the continuing life of his family.
Your four-year-old also may want to know what his future holds. He may ask when certain major events will
occur in his life.

How to Enrich Social Interaction

During this year, there are many opportunities to expand
and enrich your child's language through his social contacts. Nursery school, activity classes, special excursions,
and visits with friends are all vital to his social and intellectual growth. Your child may ask you to dial his friend's
telephone number so he can tell him about his new
goldfish. He may also want to "write" to a friend or
relative. Use pictures from an old magazine for his letter;
your child can dictate the words to you that fill in the
spaces between the pictures. Help him find pictures that
show the events he wants to talk about in his letter: "I
went to the [picture of a zoo]. I saw [pictures of various
animals]. I had [picture of hamburger and French fries]
for lunch. I got a [picture of a balloon]. I took the [pic-
ture of a bus] home."

Your four-year-old has preferences for certain people
and places. When possible, these should be respected.

However, he should also learn to be flexible and realize that he may not be able to do exactly what he wants, when he wants, and with whom he wants. Let your child know his opinions are considered, but help him understand why he can't always have his choice: "I know you want to go to dance class with Abby, but there is no more room in her group." "I know you want Gary to come to our house, but he's going to visit his grandmother today." "I know you want to go to the carnival this afternoon, but our car is at the garage being repaired."

Language develops with experiences and knowledge. An active, interesting life provides many topics for conversation, and a curious, inquiring mind equips a child to meet any and all challenges.

ADVANCED ACTIVITIES

*Sound Games

Sound Bingo helps your child remember all the sounds he's learned. When your child is familiar with enough sounds, make a Bingo card. You can start with as few as four spaces and increase the number any time by enlarging the grid. Put a letter in each box and give your child raisins or another treat to use as markers. Begin by saying the sound and having your child match the letter and mark the appropriate box. As his skill increases, say a word and ask your child to mark the box that has the same initial sound as the word. He can call out "Bingo!" when his card is full or when a specific pattern has been made. The reward for Bingo is eating the raisins. Sound

Bingo is fun for one child to play alone or for several children to play together.

Sound Riddles encourages your child to remember the initial sound in a word by answering a riddle: "I'm thinking of something that begins with the sound *m.* It's white and comes from cows." Your child then guesses, "Milk." If he needs additional clues, you might add, "Children drink it from glasses and babies drink it from bottles."

When your child is able to answer these riddles, make the game more challenging. Don't identify the initial sound: "I'm thinking of something that begins with the same sound as begins the word 'mop.' We see it in the sky at night." In this riddle, he must first figure out the sound you're referring to and then guess the answer. If he needs some extra word clues, you might say, "This sound is also at the beginning of the words 'man,' 'meet,' and 'mitten.' "

*Scrapbooks

Homonym Scrapbook. To help him understand the concept of two words with the same sound but different meanings, your child can make a scrapbook of homonyms. Explain what "homonym" means by providing examples. Illustrations of a piece of steak for "meat" and two people shaking hands for "meet" could be one example. Pictures of an airplane and some flies could show "fly" and "flies." A picture of a deer and another picture of a letter could demonstrate "deer" and "dear." Your child can try searching for just the right illustrations for the words. Some other pairs you might suggest are: ate–eight, break–brake, sun–son, write–right, mail–male, sail–sale, red–read.

Compound Words Scrapbook. Compound words are also

an interesting topic for a scrapbook. Explain to your child that these are words composed of two small words. Show him how "bedroom" is made from the little words "bed" and "room," "popcorn" contains "pop" and "corn," and "newspaper" includes "news" and "paper." Help him locate pictures for the compound words: A container of milk and a man show "milkman"; a cow and a boy represent "cowboy"; a foot and a ball depict "football"; a rainy day and a bow convey "rainbow." Perhaps you could give your child a compound word and ask him to figure out the words that make it up. The reverse process, in which he must guess the compound word based on the little words you supply, is also a good game.

My Dictionary. Your child can make a scrapbook that is his own personal dictionary. For the scrapbook, you can select pictures illustrating both familiar and unfamiliar words. If your child is interested, you could print a short definition under each picture. Even though he probably can't read the definitions, he may learn some of the words through repetition. Arrange the pictures alphabetically as in a real dictionary. It's fun to try to find a picture for each letter of the alphabet.

*Riddles

Figuring out riddles is a marvelous "mind-stretching" activity. When your child gets the answer to a riddle, he's justifiably proud. Try to find riddles on your child's level because then guessing the answer gives him a feeling of success at the same time as it forces him to think. You can also make up your own riddles by describing familiar objects: What has four legs and you sit on it? What grows and has branches instead of arms? What is furry and meows? As your child grasps the humor in many riddles, he may try his hand at creating his own. Some of them may even stump you!

*Pantomime

Explain to your child that in pantomime he's not allowed to talk, make any sounds, or use real objects as props. He must express his idea through his motions.

Begin with pantomimes of familiar situations. Suggest that he pantomime combing his hair, washing his hands, eating an ice cream cone, building a block tower, or putting on his hat. Enjoy his performance. When your child is comfortable with the technique of pantomime, encourage him to express his own ideas. You and your child can try to guess each other's pantomimes by playing a simple form of charades.

Show your child how feelings can also be communicated through pantomime. Encourage him to use his whole body, and not just his face, when he pantomimes the following suggestions: "Show me how you would feel if you got a new bicycle." "Show me how you would feel if your new bicycle broke." "Show me how you would feel if you were all alone on a dark street." "Show me how you would feel if you got sick and we had to cancel your birthday party." "Show me how you would feel after a day at the beach." These pantomimes teach your child to recognize emotions. He learns that a particular circumstance may produce a related feeling.

When your child can pantomime an individual incident or feeling, he's ready to branch out. Show him how to pantomime a series of actions that combine into an entire event. If you're pretending to prepare a meal, your actions might include opening the refrigerator, taking out the food, closing the door of the refrigerator, chopping the onions, measuring the ingredients, mixing the food, turning on the stove, putting the food in the pot, stirring the food, turning off the stove, and putting the food on a plate. Encourage your child to choose his own action to pantomime. If he can't think of one, suggest he pantomime such things as drawing a picture, opening a present, or getting dressed. Discuss the sequence of actions needed to complete the event. Compliment him on his performance and offer any constructive suggestions you may have for improving it. Perhaps he forgot to open the box of crayons, or didn't bother taking the wrapping paper off the present, or didn't button his shirt. Your remarks should be specific and encourage further attempts at pantomime. Don't stifle his creative impulses with unnecessary criticism.

What Did I Forget? can be played with pantomime. Choose a familiar activity and pantomime it for your child. Leave out one or two crucial steps, however, and ask him to tell you what you forgot. In a pantomime of taking a bath, you might omit the steps of getting undressed and turning on the water. In a pantomime of going out of the house, you might "forget" to put on your coat or open the door.

Pantomime helps your child improve his powers of observation. It also makes him more aware of actions and how they convey feelings. The ability to express oneself clearly and concisely doesn't only apply to spoken language. Remember, vast amounts of information are communicated nonverbally. Through these pantomime activities, your child develops the insight and skill needed to interpret this kind of communication. He also learns how he can use his body and face to "talk" to others. As you and your child talk about his pantomimes, his language development is also bound to be stimulated.

Appendix

How Consonant Sounds Are Produced

It's useful for parents who wish to be good speech models for their children to know not only how speech is "made," but, in particular, how consonant sounds are produced.

These sounds originate by our moving the articulators (lips, tongue, teeth, hard and soft palates) in very specific ways detailed below:

p – (voiceless) Press your lips together. Pop them open to let out a puff of air.

pail   apple   lamp

b – (voiced) Press your lips together. Pop them open to let out a puff of air. Use your voice.

boat   rabbit   knob

t – (voiceless) Press your tongue tip on the gum ridge behind your upper teeth. Keep your lips parted. Lower your tongue quickly and let out a puff of breath.

toy   little   sit

d – (voiced) Press your tongue tip on the gum ridge behind your upper teeth. Keep your lips parted. Lower your tongue quickly and let out a puff of breath. Use your voice.

doll   Indian   bread

m – (voiced) Place your lips together. Hum through your nose. This is a nasal sound.

moon   lemon   drum

n – (voiced) Press your tongue tip on the gum ridge behind your upper teeth. Hum through your nose. This is a nasal sound.

nurse   piano   sun

ng – (voiced) Lift the back of your tongue up to the soft palate. Hum through your nose. This is a nasal sound.

finger   king

wh – (voiceless) Round your lips to form a small opening. Let the air come through.

why   when   white

w – (voiced) Round your lips to form a small opening. Let air come through. Use your voice.

wood   quiet   someone

h – (voiceless) Open your mouth and let the air come out as if you were sighing or panting.

heavy   hair   hand

k – (voiceless) Lift the back of your tongue to your soft

palate. Drop your tongue quickly and let out a breath.

car   basket   book

g – (voiced) Lift the back of your tongue to your soft palate. Drop your tongue quickly and let out a breath. Use your voice.

girl   wagon   bag

y – (voiced) Raise the middle of your tongue and lower the tip behind your bottom front teeth as you would to make the *ee* sound. Use your voice.

yarn   new   Tuesday

f – (voiceless) Put your upper teeth lightly on your lower lip. Let the air come out through the opening between your teeth and lip.

fish   elephant   leaf

v – (voiced) Put your upper teeth lightly on your lower lip. Let the air come out through the opening between your teeth and lip. Use your voice.

vest   television   stove

th – (voiceless) Place the tip of your tongue lightly against your upper front teeth so that your tongue protrudes slightly. Let the air come out through the opening between your tongue and teeth.

thread   toothbrush   mouth

th – (voiced) Place the tip of your tongue lightly against your upper front teeth so that your tongue protrudes slightly. Let the air come out through the opening between your tongue and teeth. Use your voice.

this   mother   breathe

l – (voiced) Press your tongue tip on the gum ridge behind your upper teeth. Use your voice, keeping your tongue in this position.

lamp   umbrella   hill

s – (voiceless) Lift your tongue tip near the gum ridge behind your upper teeth. Widen your tongue so the sides gently touch the inside of your upper teeth. Open your teeth slightly and spread your lips in a little smile. Blow the air down a groove in the center of your tongue through the space between your tongue tip and gum ridge. This sound may also be made by placing your tongue tip near the gum ridge behind your lower teeth.

soda   pencil   dress

z – (voiced) Lift your tongue tip near the gum ridge behind your upper teeth. Widen your tongue so the sides gently touch the inside of your upper teeth. Open your teeth slightly and spread your lips in a little smile. Blow the air down a groove in the center of your tongue through the space between your tongue tip and gum ridge. Use your voice. This sound may also be made by placing your tongue tip near the gum ridge behind your lower teeth.

zebra   present   nose

sh – (voiceless) Lift your tongue tip near the gum ridge behind your upper teeth. Move your tongue back somewhat so the sides touch the inside of your upper teeth. Move your lips forward. Blow the air down the middle of your tongue.

shoe   dishes   fish

zh – (voiced) Lift your tongue tip near the gum ridge

behind your upper teeth. Move your tongue back somewhat so the sides touch the inside of your upper teeth.
Move your lips forward. Blow the air down the middle of
your tongue. Use your voice.

> division   rouge

ch – (voiceless) This sound combines the *t* and *sh*
sounds. Press your tongue tip on the gum ridge behind
your upper teeth. Move your lips forward. Remove your
tongue quickly and let out a puff of breath as you change
from the *t* to the *sh* placement.

> cheese   teacher   watch

j – (voiced) This sound combines the *d* and *zh* sounds.
Press your tongue tip on the gum ridge behind your
upper teeth. Move your lips forward. Remove your
tongue quickly and let out a puff of breath as you change
from the *d* to the *zh* placement.

> jacket   angel   bridge

r – (voiced) Lift your tongue tip and curl it slightly back
toward the top of your mouth. Curve the sides of your
tongue upward to touch the insides of your upper teeth.
Raise the back of your tongue toward your soft palate.
Use your voice.

> rain   arrow

Suggested Reading for Parents

Some of the books we've included are general child development guides. Others offer ideas for projects parents and children can work on together. Since language learning relates to all areas of your child's life, these books should be informative as well as interesting.

Becker, Wesley C., and Janis W. Becker. *Successful Parenthood.* Chicago: Follett Publishing Co., 1974.

Brazelton, T. Berry. *Toddlers and Parents.* New York: Dell Publishing Co., Inc., 1974.

————*Infants and Mothers.* New York: Delacorte Press, 1975.

Broad, Laura Peabody, and Nancy Towner Butterworth. *The Playgroup Handbook.* New York: St. Martin's Press, 1974.

Caplan, Frank and Theresa. *The Power of Play.* New York: Anchor Press/Doubleday & Co., Inc., 1973.

D'Amato, Janet and Alex. *Cardboard Carpentry.* New York: The Lion Press, 1966.

Dodson, Fitzhugh. *How to Parent.* Los Angeles: Nash Publishing, 1970.

Fiarotta, Phyllis. *Sticks and Stones and Ice Cream Cones.* New York: Workman Publishing Co., 1973.

Fraiberg, Selma. *The Magic Years.* New York: Charles Scribner's Sons, 1959.

Gordon, Thomas. *P.E.T.—Parent Effectiveness Training.* New York: Wyden Press, 1970.

Hershoff, Evelyn Glantz. *It's Fun to Make Things from Scrap Materials.* New York: Dover Publications, Inc., 1964.

Johnson, June. *Home Play for the Preschool Child.* New York: Harper & Row Publishers, 1957.

Larrick, Nancy. *A Parent's Guide to Children's Reading.* New York: Doubleday & Co., Inc., 1958.

Maynard, Fredelle. *Guiding Your Child to a More Creative Life.* New York: Doubleday & Co., Inc., 1973.

Neisser, Edith G. *Primer for Parents of Preschoolers.* New York: Parents' Magazine Press, 1972.

Pomeranz, Virginia, with Dodi Schultz. *The First Five Years.* New York: Doubleday & Co., Inc., 1973.

Rozzi, James. *Simply Fun.* New York: Parents' Magazine Press, 1968.

Salk, Lee. *What Every Child Would Like His Parents to Know*.* New York: David McKay Co., Inc., 1972.

Slade, Richard. *Carton Craft.* New York: S. G. Phillips, Inc., 1972.

Smith, Evelyn. *Nursery Rhyme Toys.* New York: Drake Publishers, 1973.

Spock, Benjamin. *Baby and Child Care.* New York: Hawthorn Books, Inc., 1976.

Wood, Katharine. *Here's How.* New York: David McKay Co., Inc., 1968.